D0367129

"If you are interested in immersing yourself in God's story and not just hooking God up to your own agenda, *Buck-Naked Faith* is for you. This book will absolutely make a difference in your capacity to grow as a Christian."

—RICH NATHAN, senior pastor, Vineyard Church of Columbus

"Eric Sandras says it straight: 'You and I are not some super church figures. We are just, well, us.' If you want a better reality, if you want hope, if you want to meet the God of ordinary people— Jesus—read this book."

—JIM HENDERSON, executive director, Off the Map,
www.off-the-map.org

A Brutally Honest Look at Stunted Christianity

ERIC SANDRAS, PH.D.

NAVPRESS®

BRINGING TRUTH TO LIFE

OUR GUARANTEE TO YOU

We believe so strongly in the message of our books that we are making this quality guarantee to you. If for any reason you are disappointed with the content of this book, return the title page to us with your name and address and we will refund to you the list price of the book. To help us serve you better, please briefly describe why you were disappointed. Mail your refund request to: NavPress, P.O. Box 35002, Colorado Springs, CO 80935.

The Navigators is an international Christian organization. Our mission is to reach, disciple, and equip people to know Christ and to make Him known through successive generations. We envision multitudes of diverse people in the United States and every other nation who have a passionate love for Christ, live a lifestyle of sharing Christ's love, and multiply spiritual laborers among those without Christ.

NavPress is the publishing ministry of The Navigators. NavPress publications help believers learn biblical truth and apply what they learn to their lives and ministries. Our mission is to stimulate spiritual formation among our readers.

© 2004 by Eric Sandras

All rights reserved. No part of this publication may be reproduced in any form without written permission from NavPress, P.O. Box 35001, Colorado Springs, CO 80935.
www.navpress.com

NAVPRESS, BRINGING TRUTH TO LIFE, and the NAVPRESS logo are registered trademarks of NavPress. Absence of ® in connection with marks of NavPress or other parties does not indicate an absence of registration of those marks.

ISBN 1-57683-525-1

Cover design by Chris Gilbert, UDG DesignWorks
Cover photo by Photonica
Creative Team: Terry Behimer, Karen Lee-Thorp, Cara Iverson, Pat Miller

Some of the anecdotal illustrations in this book are true to life and are included with the permission of the persons involved. All other illustrations are composites of real situations, and any resemblance to people living or dead is coincidental.

Song lyrics in chapter 5 are from "Be The Centre," by Michael Frye ©1999 Vineyard Songs (UK/Eire). Admin. by Vineyard Music Global worldwide. Used by permission from Vineyard Music Global, Inc., P.O. Box 68025, Anaheim, CA 92817-0825, www.VineyardMusic.com.

Unless otherwise identified, all Scripture quotations in this publication are taken from the HOLY BIBLE: NEW INTERNATIONAL VERSION® (NIV®). Copyright © 1973, 1978, 1984 by International Bible Society. Used by permission of Zondervan Publishing House. All rights reserved. Other versions used include: the *Revised Standard Version Bible* (RSV), copyright 1946, 1952, 1971, by the Division of Christian Education of the National Council of the Churches of Christ in the USA, used by permission, all rights reserved.

Sandras, Eric, 1965-
 Buck-naked faith : a brutally honest look at Christianity / Eric Sandras.
  p. cm.
 Includes bibliographical references and index.
 ISBN 1-57683-525-1
 1. Christian life. I. Title.
 BV4501.3.S27 2004
 248.4--dc22

2004002724

Printed in Canada

2 3 4 5 6 7 8 9 10 / 08 07 06 05 04

FOR A FREE CATALOG OF NAVPRESS BOOKS & BIBLE STUDIES,
CALL 1-800-366-7788 (USA) OR 1-416-499-4615 (CANADA)

Although many have influenced this kid to grow, few have shaped my life more than these men and women, whom I call my mentors: Rick O., Bruce F., Ed C., Marty S., Todd H., Dave P., Grandpa C., Mom, and Dad. May my own children be so blessed.

To my friends who have decided with me that becoming an authentic follower of Christ is more than rhetoric but instead a lifelong pursuit.

To my wife, Cynthia, whose love I hold more precious than anything.

CONTENTS

FOREWORD

IN THIS HINGE PERIOD of history that we call the postmodern era, many of us yearn to drop the pretense. The modern period taught us to be unreal. From Descartes to modern time, we were told we were the center of our own universe, so we tried to live as the gods of our little worlds. We put on artificial faces and played games. We dressed ourselves to look successful. We hid our despair, shame, and weakness—we had no room for them. If we were going to rule our little universe, we had to do it from a position of strength. If we hadn't made it yet, the game was to "fake it till we make it."

Modern spirituality was not much better. Even people in the church put on masks and played games. Our language became filled with religious babble. We acted as if we were perfect saints, though our lives gave little evidence of that high calling. We looked nice, dressed right, talked the talk, but something was wrong and we all knew it. Our religiosity felt empty.

But things are changing in the postmodern world. Today's eclectic nonphilosophy is sowing many things that we might abhor into the minds of Western thinkers, but one thing for which we can be thankful is a reawakened yearning for something real. We're tired of artificiality, in architecture and relationships. We're bypassing the glitz and show of modernism. There is a cry to go back to the ancient paths—back to the classics, back to the time when things were really what they appeared to be.

Eric Sandras taps into this need for genuine friendship with Christ and calls us to make the pursuit of it our life's pilgrimage. With a penitent openness, he takes off the mask and bares his life for all to see. I have seen Eric's willingness to be vulnerable as he pastors a church and coaches church planters in the movement I lead. Something rings true here—something of sterling character as he openly shares both his strengths and his failures.

Eric returns to the spirituality of the mystics and other church leaders of the past. Letting them speak in a fresh way, Eric points out signposts that will direct us into the future.

The spirituality he calls for here does not take us on a solo journey. Eric recognizes the absolute importance of living in a community where people are honest with one another and working side by side to follow God's call. We didn't think we needed community in the modern world. We believed we could make it on our own. But throughout the history of the church, genuine spirituality has always been nurtured in the womb of genuine Christian community. Eric helps us gain a fresh hold on this ancient truth.

Buck-Naked Faith is one pilgrim's attempt to call his fellow pilgrims back toward the real deal. I encourage you to join him. You will like the result.

BERTEN WAGGONER
national director,
The Association of Vineyard Churches— USA

CHAPTER 1

BRUTALLY HONEST

SEX WITH A STRANGER wasn't supposed to end this way. I hadn't gone into this evening wanting my two worlds to collide. But by midnight my fantasy life was going to ensure that my spiritual life would begin to crumble.

I had worked hard to make sure I met this girl in a place where my Christian friends didn't hang out. The odds were totally in my favor (at least until you factor in the Holy Spirit). I attended a university with over sixteen thousand students. What was the chance that one girl at one remote college hangout would know me—the other me?

It wasn't like I went to that club just looking for sex. I think what I really wanted was a bit of a reprieve from my everyday life. I just wanted to get away from having to be so "nice" for a while. I felt I deserved it. After all, I was a full-time student, worked on the side as a waiter, and led a student ministry boasting over 250 people in attendance. Around campus I felt I always needed to live up to the image of being a spiritual leader. I had a responsibility to the troops to live a godly life—the whole live-above-reproach thing. My social world on campus surrounded me with the expectation that I walk the talk.

No doubt I was sincere in my concern for the lost, my desire to inspire others to become disciples of Jesus, and my love for God. I really did care about these things and about honoring God with my life. Yet periodically I found myself drawn to the freedom of not being known for any of this stuff. I just wanted the opportunity to live my life (at least for an evening) without having to measure up to some unattainable standard. Like the token heathens I evangelized, I occasionally wanted to enjoy the benefits of the opposite sex without all the responsibility my faith and morality attached to them. It was sometimes appealing to indulge my flesh just a little bit, at least so I knew what I was missing the other eighty-five days of the semester. My periodic desire to escape was only superceded by my need to return unscathed and undiscovered.

God had a different agenda that night. He was going to invade my private world and shake it to its core. From this moment on, my soul would be scarred. I would forever know that the painful consequences of duplicity far outweigh its benefits.

Five Life-Changing Words

The dagger came as I smugly rolled over in bed, feeling pretty good about my performance and slightly enjoying the rush that accompanies risks like I was taking. Then I noticed some tears welling up in the girl's eyes. They weren't tears of joy or even deep hurt; they were tears of disappointment. This became even more evident in the five words that accompanied those drops of disillusionment: "I thought you were different."

It was like someone had just unzipped the covering off a black hole in my soul. I felt my world implode. "I thought you were different." Those words echoed inside my hollow character.

But unlike an echo, the words seemed to grow in force until every corner of my darkened understanding was awakened.

Suddenly, I realized that I did indeed know this woman, who hours ago had only been the target of my carnal desires. How could I have been so blind? She had just started attending the weekly campus meetings of our university fellowship. She was simply trying to make sense out of Christianity and religion. In *my* eyes she had only been an object of my attraction, but in *her* eyes I had been Jesus.

Obviously, she was having trouble reconciling the Jesus in me she witnessed at our Wednesday night gatherings and the Jesus in me she had just slept with. One wanted to give her everything and save her life; the other wanted to take something from her and steal her life. A divine spotlight was shining in that room, and the sinner being exposed was me.

Now, don't get me wrong. It is not like I woke up one day and decided to live a life of duplicity. It's not like I decided to fake my way through Christianity. Quite the contrary, I honestly thought I was doing pretty well. After all, people were coming to Christ, I was teaching the Bible with a competent level of gifting, and those around me constantly told me I was spiritual. But time had produced a widening gap between my external profession and my internal character. Those things I claimed to believe and do were far exceeding my reality.

Have you been there? Around one group you profess to believe and do so much more than your life indicates, yet something inside knows you are being and acting deceitfully.

Suddenly I knew I needed help. I finally admitted that something was tragically wrong, yet I didn't know how to fix it. Thankfully, I knew someone who did. But it meant being brutally honest, ending my charade, and submitting to someone I trusted.

Gifts Versus Character

I walked into Pastor Rick's office the next day after a night of sleepless torment. I knew that trying to fix this problem on my own had only led to more duplicity. I needed a mentor. Rick had been my pastor for years, but I had never seen the need to be transparent around him. I had wanted his approval and his recognition of God's work in my life more than his wisdom and character development.

Deep inside, I was afraid that if he learned about the black hole in my character, I would lose what superficial connection I had with him. But in order to escape the trap of duplicity, desperation must become more important than image. I knew I really loved God and wanted to find meaning and purpose in my walk with Jesus; however, I felt I was on the verge of disqualification. Little did I realize that my crisis was actually bringing me to the brink of what my spirit truly longed for—a cooperative friendship with Jesus.

Now, there's a fifteen-dollar bit of religious rhetoric that could have carried a whole trainload of momentum in my life had I truly understood it. Deep down I wanted to be the type of person who, like Jesus' closest disciples, could walk the dusty roads of life with him—growing in my understanding of his kingdom, his power, his authority, *and* his person. I knew it would be incredible to have Jesus share with me not only the power of his creativity but also the humor. It was one thing to trust Jesus enough to tell him how I felt, but it would be something entirely different when he trusted me enough to tell me how he felt. What I didn't realize then was that the path to that kind of friendship runs through the valley of brokenness.

So there I was—disillusioned, damaged, and disqualified. What I thought could be the end of my spiritual career was actually just the beginning of learning to be a genuine apprentice to the Master.

Jesus was about to lead me through a fifteen-year training course so that I could truly become who I professed to be. And though I didn't see him then, Jesus was there at every step.

Pastor Rick listened as I unloaded my sin, fears, and shame. It was as if he had been waiting for this moment. Gently he said, "Perhaps it's time for the Lone Ranger to become a part of the team. I can help you, but for you it won't be easy. For starters, I want you to resign from leadership and cancel all of your speaking engagements for the next six months."

Inside my head the battle began to rage. *What? Are you crazy? I was asking for help, not martyrdom. I have a responsibility to all these people. They need my leadership and inspiration. Can't we work on me while I stay involved with them?* I had so many questions, so many justifications as to why I shouldn't be transparent and broken further.

Pastor Rick answered them all with one simple statement: "How bad do you want to be whole?"

For the first time in my life, I began to learn the difference between character and giftedness. (Later in this book we will explore that topic further.) Apprenticeship led me to a place of healing the deeper wounds in my life. It was a frustrating process filled with as much pain and embarrassment as success and security. Often the temporary satisfaction of minimizing my flaws and maximizing my giftedness seemed appealing, but then Pastor Rick's wisdom would push me further: "Eric, God doesn't build a man, he breaks him."

So as you read this book and grow in living what you profess, perhaps you will feel the breaking. Then again, maybe you are already so offended by my past that you can't see your own present. Jesus' healing and forgiveness have been so powerful and redeeming in my life that I've got nothing to lose these days. I don't have a reputation to maintain, only a love to live.

Not There Yet

Of course, twenty-one years into my walk with Jesus, it would sure seem that my character would be perfected, but it isn't. Still, somehow in this conversion process it has become as easy for me—well, almost—to share my weaknesses and sin as it is my strengths and passions. I say almost, because even as I sit here in the Bella Rosa Cafe, my favorite local coffee shop, I find myself feeling strangely vulnerable. As I pound the keys on my laptop, I keep looking over my shoulder, hoping nobody is reading the stuff I just wrote.

Nonetheless, I'll share my failures and successes with you, hoping that you'll pray for me and give me grace as I now walk with a spiritual limp. In return, I will give you permission to be honest. Read slowly and find those areas in which you profess one thing but find yourself living another. It is in those areas of tension that you might actually find God pulling you toward his future and not yours.

Sometimes moments of tension are actually God's grace leading us to a crisis of decision. Still, we both know that Jesus can lead sheep like us to water, but he can't make us drink.

There Must Be More

One of my deepest temptations is to practice a lifestyle that appears to be a faithful friendship with Christ but really isn't. To be a Cheese Puff Christian—lots of volume but little substance. Cheese puffs take up space in the bowl, but crush them and you're lucky to get a tablespoon of substance out of them. Likewise, it's so easy to puff up my life with religious air without much of the kingdom that Jesus was passionate about bringing. To be in a cooperative friendship with Christ means to enter into his story and live life on behalf of his kingdom, his agenda in the world. Unfortunately, life has a way of exposing who I really am—a real friend of Christ, or just another religious poser.

I have had to take a brutally honest look at my life. I may be just one small grape in this diverse fruit salad we call Western culture, but I still want to be a real one. Yet I'm immersed in a world where everything is becoming virtual, instant, and shamelessly void of depth. Plastic fruit comes from a mold and only looks like it has substance; real fruit comes from the DNA given to it by its Creator. To reach its potential, it must be given time to grow to ripeness.

Have I measured the genuineness of my faith by how well I'm performing, or by how well Jesus and I are doing? Am I willing to admit that in a world of marshmallow spirituality my faith and relationship with Jesus the Master may be lacking? Something in my spirit keeps crying out, "There must be more!"

I don't want my faith to *resemble* the real thing; I want it to *be* the real thing. I don't want to preach sermons, share with others, or counsel myself regarding a God I profess to know without answering some hard questions about my spiritual life.

Towering Trees or Dusty Bushes

Not long ago while waiting for my daughter to check out books at our local library, I came across a book on bonsai gardening. It was sitting on the display shelf by the front counter, just waiting for an anxious father like me to pick it up and waste some time. Hmmm . . . bonsai gardening. You've probably seen these tiny trees, exquisite in their windswept appearance. As beautiful as they are, though, I can't help seeing the similarity of the Japanese art of bonsai and the approach to Christian faith that constantly tempts me.

Bonsai trees are intended to look like the real trees you would find outdoors. They appear to be weathered over time, able to bear fruit, healthy, and strong. The problem is that bonsai trees are stunted, contrived, and internally very weak renditions of the trees God intended them to be. If you expect a bonsai to bear fruit, you'll be disappointed. And if you place a bonsai outdoors in the rain— never mind snow and wind—it will die.

The prophet Jeremiah spoke of our choice to become bonsai or grow tall:

"Cursed is the one who trusts in man,
> who depends on flesh for his strength
> and whose heart turns away from the LORD.
He will be like a bush in the wastelands;
> he will not see prosperity when it comes.
He will dwell in the parched places of the desert,
> in a salt land where no one lives.
But blessed is the man who trusts in the LORD,
> whose confidence is in him.
He will be like a tree planted by the water
> that sends out its roots by the stream.
It does not fear when heat comes;
> its leaves are always green.
It has no worries in a year of drought
> and never fails to bear fruit." (Jeremiah 17:5-8)

Imagine with me a weathered and aged spruce tree standing alone in a backdrop of gray. Its trunk is twisted and apparently windswept; its foliage is a deep, rich green. Now in your mind's eye, pan back a little to give the tree some perspective. Realize that it is not standing in a forest but in a small container. The tree is not mighty in height or breadth but is actually quite small. It is not a *real* mighty spruce but a contrived miniature version—a bonsai.

Taking time to get a different perspective on our lives can often help us realize that what we think we're seeing in the mirror is actually only a small and struggling version of what God intends us to be. I don't want to be a bonsai believer, one who only looks like I've weathered the storms of life and faith. I want to be the real thing, growing mightily or maybe just awkwardly toward my full God-oriented potential. But to know who I am becoming requires an honest assessment and a larger perspective than many of us have ever had. Perspective often comes by standing still and getting a God's-eye view of our lives.

As we take time to stand and look at our lives, we often notice that God has placed a choice in front of us. Do we want to continue to pursue the candy-coated, pretend-everything-is-fine faith that we've been walking aimlessly in, or do we want to pursue faith that not only bears the weight of our own lives but also permeates the lives around us?

Substantive faith can be as simple as responding with the truth instead of "fine" when someone asks how we're doing. It includes the quest of finding and fulfilling our God-given calls. It's spending on behalf of the poor instead of spending on oneself until poor. It's moving beyond "What can I get from Jesus' kingdom?" to "What can Jesus' kingdom get from me?"

Bonsai: The Scary Reality

Think for a moment: What could be one of the scariest verses in the Bible for those who profess faith in Jesus?

I remember one spoken by the Master himself to a crowd that easily could have contained you or me. The verse sends a shiver through my bones because it makes me realize that Jesus the Master can tell the difference between what I profess and who I really am.

Jesus said it this way:

"Not everyone who says to me, 'Lord, Lord,' will enter
the kingdom of heaven, but only he who does the will
of my Father who is in heaven. Many will say to me
on that day, 'Lord, Lord,' did we not prophesy in your
name, and in your name drive out demons and perform many miracles?' Then I will tell them plainly, 'I
never knew you. Away from me, you evildoers!'"
(Matthew 7:21-23)

Oh, how close to true spirituality I have often come without
grasping its fundamental requirement: relationship with Jesus the
Master. I often wonder, *Have I subtly misinterpreted the Father's
will as works when his intention is relationship?* I'm talking about
a real, interactive relationship through the tangible person of
Jesus Christ.

The word *knew* in Matthew 7:23 can be paralleled with Genesis
2:24-25, where Adam and Eve are to be one flesh and are unashamed
of their nakedness. In essence, we shouldn't hide anything—God
wants us buck naked. Do I know Jesus like I know my wife? Better
yet, does Jesus know me like I know my wife? It sounds strange,
but does Jesus see me as his intimate partner, or just a guy who's
only interested in the bennies of dating?

Let's go a bit further. Tie Matthew 7:24 in with the preceding
thoughts and we find that putting Jesus' words into practice is more
about loving him passionately than about obedience to rules:

"Therefore everyone who hears these words of mine
and puts them into practice is like a wise man who
built his house on the rock." (Matthew 7:24)

What does Jesus mean by "puts [his words] into practice"? Most of us have been trained to read his words as rules and doctrine first, believing that obedience to the externals of those rules will produce goodness inside us. But if we focus on being obedient in the externals, we remain hollow internally. We orient our lives around the *effects* of God's kingdom—being good, not telling outright lies, not cheating on our spouse, writing a check to feed the poor—and not the core of the kingdom—loving the Lord our God with all of our heart, soul, and mind (see Matthew 22:37-39). Yet if we truly invest in making sure that our core is right, the godly behaviors will flow naturally from that place. It's possible to gather around another's fire and get warm, but true relationship has the fire coming from within.

Remember Jeremiah's admonishment about shriveled bushes or growing trees? We all have an important choice to make. Do we want to be a bush in the wasteland, or would we rather be a fearless tree by the stream? In other words, are we willing to work toward abundant life, or do we just give up and default to bonsai?

One thing that the towering tree and tiny bonsai have in common is time—neither of them got that way overnight. In a world of artificial sweeteners, pseudo-intimacy via the Net, virtual airplane rides, and silicone body parts, I've found something real. It's not some secret formula or thirty-day money-back guarantee to sainthood, but it is some insight into the only person who has ever fully lived what we blithely call a "relationship with God": Jesus Christ. Maybe you will find, as I have, that it is the *pursuit* of the kind of relationship with the Father that Jesus had, and not the expectation of attainment in this lifetime, that we've needed all along.

Binging and Purging

Let's hear that again: Maybe it is the pursuit of this type of relationship with God, and not the expectation of attainment, that we've needed all along. Let this idea tweak your doctrinal monoliths if it has to.

Every person, every church, every denomination, and every culture that professes to be Christian builds doctrinal systems. When they grow from mere rhetoric to behavior-changing beliefs, that's great. But often those beliefs harden into inflexible dogma and ultimately become a biblically substantiated, faith-propping, surrogate relationship with God. Subtly our doctrines become more important than living what our doctrines originally meant. For example, we've learned we are "saved by grace through faith"! But what does that mean for us today? The truth we think we have discovered becomes more important than continuing to discover truth. Like Grandpa's ashes in the urn above the fireplace, it has no life in itself, but we don't feel right about throwing it away.

Our relationship with God isn't the ultimate knowing of some static set of beliefs. It is fluid, dynamic, and often counterintuitive. Like a river flowing uphill, winding its way toward heaven, we aren't there yet, but we can know we're heading in the right direction.

For example, perhaps like me you've tried and tried to live under Jesus' command to "be perfect, therefore, as your heavenly Father is perfect" (Matthew 5:48). But hearing that command through a westernized theological filter, you've taken it to mean that you must be perfect *now*. So you end up in bulimic Christianity.

You try really, really hard to be good and pure and holy—then you give up and fall into temptation. But since you are falling, you might as well do it big. Then, when the guilt and emptiness of what you've done settles in, you go and get a good old-fashioned cleansing from the Holy Spirit.

We all know the cycle. Sin, repent, sin, repent, sin, repent—the cycle continues until we either give up trying to be "good" or we become the old crusty believers who may not be doing "bad" things anymore but sure don't show the passion for life and humanity that true goodness from Jesus brings.

What are the things that you tend to binge and purge on? Depression, lust, ESPN, romance novels, food, Xbox, chat rooms— the list of our personal bulimic vices is almost endless.

Did I touch on a favorite? Have you given up fighting the urge when it comes? Have you found yourself becoming legalistic and judgmental toward the bingers around you in order to feel more righteous yourself?

If, like me, you can say yes to any or all of those questions, then you should now ask, "Jesus, is there a good way to grow that takes me away from a life of pretending, toward real goodness and holiness?"

Perpetual Progress Is the Key

Church father Gregory of Nyssa (approximately AD 331-396) seemed to have understood that the willingness to pursue friendship with God yields more benefit than pretending to have already attained it. He grasped that it is in the struggle of pursuit that we grow closer to that friendship. The perpetual progress we make toward real intimacy, empowered by God's grace and motivated by our Father's relentless love, becomes more important than the final outcome. In "The Life of Moses," Gregory writes,

> Since the goal of the virtuous way of life is the very
> thing we have been seeking, it is time for you, noble
> friend, to be known by God and to become his friend.

This is true perfection: not to avoid a wicked life because like slaves we severely fear punishment, not to do good because we hope for rewards. . . . On the contrary, disregarding all those things for which we hope and which have been reserved by promise, we regard falling from God's friendship as the only thing dreadful and we consider becoming God's friend the only thing worthy of honor and desire. This, as I have said, is the perfection of life.[1]

Wow! Becoming God's friend. *Becoming* God's friend. There's a process in there somewhere. Gregory knows we fall away and draw close. Friendship is like that; slavery is not. Being a slave is a static position—all that changes is your performance and punishments. Friendship has the potential to grow deeper or shallower depending on the efforts of those involved.

If I see my relationship with Christ as only a business transaction (he paid for my sin and I agree to his four-spiritual-laws contract), I'm stuck. I'll spend the rest of my days living up to the contract. However, if I enter into this relationship as a friendship, the depth and potential of that relationship is as infinite as the person with whom I'm engaging.

Now, *that* is the direction I would like to grow all the days of my life—having substance in my relationship with God! Could what I profess to have and what I actually experience become one and the same? I sure hope so. Thus, pursuing friendship becomes not only the goal but also the process. Of course, you could settle for the surreal bliss of the superficial if that's all your soul truly longs for—in which case, the ancient bonsai tradition will be all you ever need.

It Starts with Just a Seed

Are you heading toward realness, or bonsaihood? One way to tell is by the place the kingdom of God holds in your life. Jesus said that from its beginning as a tiny seed, the kingdom must grow both internally and externally in our lives:

> He told them another parable: "The kingdom of heaven is like a mustard seed, which a man took and planted in his field. Though it is the smallest of all your seeds, yet when it grows, it is the largest of garden plants and becomes a tree, so that the birds of the air come and perch in its branches."
>
> He told them still another parable: "The kingdom of heaven is like yeast that a woman took and mixed into a large amount of flour until it worked all through the dough." (Matthew 13:31-33)

The kingdom of God should produce long-term consequences out of proportion to its insignificant beginnings in our lives. The mustard seed suggests extensive growth (growing big on the outside) and the yeast suggests intensive growth (growing big on the inside).

Like yeast in dough, the kingdom needs to permeate every aspect of our being. Some have taught, with validity, to interpret the birds and the yeast negatively, as symbols of evil. However, as he often did, Jesus may have purposely used these metaphors to cause people to look deeper into what he was saying.

It's not uncommon for metaphors to have diverse uses: the lion at different places in the Bible symbolizes Satan, then Jesus; the coming of the kingdom is described as a thief in the night. So what may be most important for our discussion here is, *Are we stunting or fostering the kingdom's expansion in our lives, both internally and externally?* In other words, *Is the life we are living making us more prone to becoming bonsai believers, or true ones?*

I understand how easily my soul withers even when I want it to bear fruit. Jesus made it clear that the kingdom begins in us as a seed. Our choices unlock or hinder its growth potential. To choose the bonsai life means to deny the abundant one. Likewise, to choose the abundant life that friendship with Jesus offers means we unleash the kingdom growth potential within and turn from the principles that create a bonsai.

It Can Happen to the "Best" of Us

We have seen those who cash in on creating the bonsai life in others. They woo us with their glamorous stories of spiritual power and profession while cashing our checks. Ironically, many of those who taught us to toe the line spiritually and morally are later charged with sexual misconduct, embezzlement of monies intended for the poor, or trading in their wives for younger models. But they seemed so holy, so knowledgeable, and so saintly. What went wrong?

Did they just wake up one day and decide to choose the wrong path? More important, how can we tell if we're on a similar road to embarrassment and destruction? When we examine the extreme hypocritical lifestyles of once-lofty superstars of ministry, it's hard to understand how they could ever land so far from genuine faith.

The change often begins with a lifestyle that encourages the appearance of being God's friend without the inner passion and tough choices. As I paged through that book on bonsai gardening, I found seven simple principles that produce a successful bonsai:

1. Start with potential.
2. Pick an attractive pot.
3. Prepare the soil.
4. Limit the water supply.
5. Aim for predictability.
6. Prune excess growth.
7. Protect the tree from hardship.

Then, in one of those moments you wish you had more often, I realized those same principles were exactly what would encourage that hypocritical, stunted lifestyle I wanted to escape. Unfortunately, I also saw how those same seven principles—appealing, yet stunting—were already at work in me and others around me.

It was then that I understood: If I wanted to live in such a way that my godward DNA would reach its fullest potential, I would have to learn to live in a spirit *opposite* to that of the bonsai. So I took the seven principles, turned them 180 degrees, and came up with principles for growing a butt-kicking, life-giving friendship with Jesus:

1. Wake up your potential.
2. Embrace the power of community.
3. Enrich the soil of your life.
4. Feel the full reign of God.
5. Unleash your God-given DNA.
6. Call forth life and growth in yourself and others.
7. Learn to embrace pain.

As you read the next seven chapters, use these principles to evaluate your life. Get buck naked with Jesus—and yourself. Determine whether you are being stunted into a bonsai, or thriving with kingdom vitality.

Jesus is the Master Gardener. Let him examine your soil and branches. Trust that he has your best interests in heart as he speaks to you.

GROWTH POINTS

1. Friendship with God. What a concept. On a piece of paper or in a journal, list three specific things in your life that would change if you were cultivating your friendship with God.

2. Sit down with a cup of coffee and give yourself permission to be honest. Write down four things that you tend to binge and purge on. Are they "God" things, or "sin" things? How are they related? When do they occur? Embrace the pain.

CHAPTER 2

WAKE UP YOUR POTENTIAL

I OFTEN LOOK AT my life and realize how little fruit I've borne, how spiritually stunted I feel, and how narrow my kingdom experiences have been. "Lord, I don't want to be a bonsai believer!" my heart cries. "Empower me with your Spirit to grow!"

It seems every time I pray that prayer, he answers it and I get to grow a little more in his presence. Often that growth occurs when I step out of my own small story and risk being a part of God's larger one.

Living the Wrong Story

Recently, I met a guy named Mitch. It seems a girl he liked had badgered him into going to church. He had no desire to go, but he said he'd go once just to get her off his back. I didn't get a chance to meet him at church the Sunday he attended, but the note his girlfriend left on my desk that day prompted me to give him a call.

The note said, "Please call Mitch. He wants to meet with you about God before he goes back to prison this week."

Now *there's* something you don't see on your desk every day. So I called him, and we met at my normal coffee hangout, the Bella Rosa. Mitch was in his late forties. One look at his arms let me know he must have had a great relationship with an over-caffeinated tattoo artist. His long gray hair accentuated his quintessential biker-gang dress code.

I love all types of people, and Mitch was no exception. However, I must admit that part of me was relieved we were meeting in a public place, so other customers could come to my rescue if need be.

After some introductory small talk, I finally asked Mitch why he and I were meeting. He pushed his double cappuccino aside, leaned over the table, and said, "Listen, I don't know if you do drugs or not . . . "

Quietly but firmly I responded, "Uh, no, I don't do drugs, Mitch."

"But you know when you take a hit of some really strong *(insert biker expletive here)*, what a rush it is?"

Sheepishly I said, "Uh, no, Mitch, I don't."

"Well, anyway," Mitch continued, "when I walked in the doors of your church the other day, that's the feeling that hit me. I just want you to tell me what it was that gave me such a rush." He went on to explain that whatever happened to him that morning prompted him to make a commitment to turn himself in that week on several outstanding warrants. He knew it would mean more time in prison, but somehow he also knew it was the right thing to do. Before he went back in though, he wanted to meet with me so I could explain this strange sensation to him.

"Well, Mitch, I think what you encountered was the presence of God. There is a real need in our lives that many of us try to fill with counterfeit things like drugs and sex. But I think you encountered the real Jesus, and now you're changing. But first, why don't you tell me what you think about God."

Mitch went on to explain that he believed in God, but after what happened to his parents in a church when he was twelve, he swore he would never set foot in a church building again. There was a lot of hurt in his eyes, but he didn't give me the details. Then he spent the next half hour explaining his theory of spirituality.

It was tough to track, but Mitch felt that somehow God has this big scale, and on it he puts all the things you have done with good motives on one side, and things done with bad motives on the other. Because God is just, if the scale tips toward the good side, you are in heaven when you die, and if it tips the other way, you're out. As his explanation continued, I began to wonder if he wasn't so much trying to convert me as he was working hard to convince himself he had it figured out.

When he was through, I pushed *my* double cappuccino aside, leaned over the table, and simply asked, "Mitch, that's great, but has your philosophy gotten you where you want to be in life?"

Suddenly, this Hell's Angels poster child began to cry. "No," he said. "I know something's not right."

"Perhaps," I said, "you're living the wrong story. What if you could live the story God has for your life?"

I pulled out my Bible and read Jeremiah's classic passage: "'For I know the plans I have for you,' declares the LORD, 'plans to prosper you and not to harm you, plans to give you hope and a future'" (Jeremiah 29:11).

"Is that the story you would like to be living, Mitch?" I asked gently.

Mitch's eyes lit up and he slammed his hand down on the table. "*(Insert biker expletive here)*, yeah!" he shouted. "But it's not like anyone ever wrote a book about it!"

As I regained my composure, I pointed to my Bible and said, "God wrote a book about it. It's right here, Mitch. This is the big story that God invites you to be a part of. He wrote the book and wants to author your life as well."

Mitch is out of prison now, having served his time. He is a young believer, pretty rough around the edges, but working hard to be a follower of Christ. In many ways, he is more real in his friendship with God than you or I could ever hope to be. He's not tainted by religious mores and dogma. He feels no need to pretend to be something he has not yet become nor hide behind something he used to be. Instead, every day is a new discovery about how to merge his life into God's story.

Have you met people like Mitch, who seem to be living the wrong story? As they share their frustration and pain, I often say, "You've been living the wrong story. God does care about your life and wants to rewrite the ending that you assume is coming." Circumstances don't always change, but Jesus gives us the chance to see the story from his perspective. He invites us to leave behind our bonsai perspective and unleash our growth potential by understanding his perspective.

Stunting Our Growth Potential

In bonsai horticulture it's essential to pick a tree with lots of potential to grow—and then stunt that growth. I've seen a picture of a juniper tree that towered to three feet after nearly 150 years of life! The key is potential: either in height, trunk strength, or ability to bear fruit. Starting there, the gardener carefully denies the tree's essence.

That's the opposite of how the kingdom of God is supposed to develop in our lives. The kingdom may start off as small as a mustard seed, but given time and the right opportunities, it should grow way out of proportion to that unnoticeable beginning.

The potential we pack has more to do with God's presence working within and through us than with how qualified we feel. When we grasp the truth that we can become colaborers with Jesus and learn to live a much bigger story than our own microfocused lives, we will grow and grow and grow. God's purpose for us is to be well-watered trees that tower on the banks of his river of life.

That sounds good on paper, but then I think of my life. How much potential I have in God's kingdom! Paul's words rattle around in my often-shallow soul: "For we are God's workmanship, created in Christ Jesus to do good works, which God prepared in advance for us to do" (Ephesians 2:10).

Am I doing those good works? Shouldn't a guy twenty years into his faith be strong enough not to fear the portal of lust that he can access via the Internet? By now, shouldn't I trust God's provision enough not to worry whether or not he will provide the income for my kids to go to the dentist this month? Twenty years of potential later, shouldn't my heart be consumed with the things of Jesus and not of *me?* Instead, I often feel that my heart looks like one of those compressed spongy creatures that is supposed to grow to fifty times its size if placed in water for a few hours. My heart needs more Living Water!

God created me to play a crucial part in his huge story. But so often, I stunt my growth and try to live a microstory of my own making. Why do I do that? Why do I get distracted by my minuscule story? In part, the world teaches me to do it.

Small Stories, Big Stories

Early in his administration, President George W. Bush had his presidential mettle tested when a U.S. spy plane had to make an emergency landing in China. The Chinese held twenty-four American crewmembers in custody. The news channels buzzed with live coverage, expert opinions, and man-on-the-street perspectives.

I was particularly amused by one scene. An expert in foreign affairs explained the importance of understanding the cultural differences between our nations, the fragile relationships that had been built during the Clinton era, and the potential risks to crew members if a rescue was to be attempted. Then the scene cut to some guy on the street who was walking an impatient, junkyard-looking dog. While the canine pulled on his leash, this gentleman shared his opinion: "Let's just send some navy SEALs over there, shoot anyone who gets in the way, and bring our boys home." What caught my attention was that somehow, in the larger presentation of this newscast, it appeared that Junkyard Bob's opinion was just as valid as the foreign affairs expert's.

Now here is the rub. Most of us would say Bob's opinion is valid, but I wonder, does that necessarily mean it's relevant or accurate? I hear many people today talking about how *metanarratives* are oppressive. A metanarrative is a larger story that explains the big picture of what's going on. If metanarratives are out, micronarratives are in. And as I listen, I hear everyone wanting to tell *his or her own* story. Somehow, in our culture, everyone's opinion has become important and equal.

Riding the wave of our insatiable need to be significant, we seem to be saying, "My experiences, my story, my understanding of God and reality are just as valid as anyone else's." Now hold on there, Hoss. Even Jesus'? Am I not safe to assume that Jesus, being God's one and only Son, knows a lot about religion, faith, and the worship experience? If Jesus is the Master of Life, he seems qualified to grab a bit more airtime than Bob or me.

Jesus is the expert on the metanarrative and the micronarrative.

He understands the overall story and how my story fits into his Book of Life. It's not all about me. Bonsai faith needs me to make my story look big. A faith in which I'm working together with Jesus needs me to see my story as part of his. It urges me to discover how my story reflects and connects with the overarching story of a just and gracious God, who throughout history has loved and sought after a rebellious humanity—and more specifically, a rebellious man named Eric.

So the quest is to avoid losing the awesome larger story under an inflated sense of our own story's importance. I want to merge my story into his. Then the kingdom of God expands in my life and my potential is unleashed. We followers of Christ have such potential to participate in something much bigger than ourselves. We can live the bonsai life, in which we know our potential yet live constricted stories with an exaggerated sense of importance, or we can release our full potential by learning to move in harmony with God's kingdom.

Ask yourself, *Whose opinions get more airtime during my prayer time: mine or Jesus'?*

Living the Larger Story

As I write this chapter, I'm sitting in a highway diner in Butte, Montana. I'm on my way back from Colorado to Washington State, trying to get home to my family and in time to prepare a sermon for Sunday. Yesterday, as my Ford Explorer was climbing a mountain pass and pulling a U-Haul trailer loaded with some furniture from my grandparents, smoke started billowing from underneath my rig. As the road behind me filled with my blue smog, I found myself going slower and slower, frantically looking for a place to pull over. The semitrucks that I so smugly passed a few moments earlier appeared in my rearview mirror like the T. rex chasing our friends in *Jurassic Park.* Just as I was losing all power, I found a wide shoulder area and pulled over.

The thoughts that went through my mind weren't what you'd expect from someone claiming to be a friend of Jesus. Perhaps Mitch's grasp of our language's creative expletives had rubbed off on me. Still, after my initial surge of useless whining, I had to ask myself some profound questions, like *How am I going get home by tomorrow?* and *How in the world am I going to pay for this?*

As the temperature in my soul cooled, I got out of the car, saw the transmission oil dripping from beneath my Explorer, and called my wife. I sat down and asked myself *Now what?* Then a strange thought entered my head: *Be a part of the story, Eric.*

Okay, I'll play. I knew I was looking at a couple thousand dollars for a new transmission, missing church on Sunday, and not getting the hugs today from my kids I was hoping for, but I decided to get radical and actually prayed. "Jesus, we've been dialoguing a lot lately about your helping me to see the larger story you are writing in my life. I do not like this chapter a whole lot right now, but I do trust you. I choose to let you be the Master of my life right now. Let me live in your story."

One hour later, the tow truck from my auto service arrived. Together the twenty-three-year-old tow-truck driver and I loaded up the Explorer and hitched up my U-Haul to begin the twenty-mile drive to Butte. *Choose wisely, Eric. Either sulk in your frustration and despair over your diminishing bank account, or look for the larger story.* This time, I chose to be an apprentice to Jesus.

Phil, the driver, muttered something about how his wife and he were just getting ready to watch Monday Night Football together when he got the call to come pick me up. "No way," I replied. "That was my goal tonight too. I was trying to get to a hotel in time to catch the game myself. Being originally from Colorado, I love to watch the Broncos play."

"Cool. We moved from Colorado just a couple of years ago," came the reply.

"Really?" I responded, sensing God was up to something. "What got you here?"

Phil went on to share with me how they had gotten married a couple of years ago in Colorado and moved to Butte so he could work on the volunteer fire department and gain experience. Now he had two on-call jobs to juggle: the tow company and the fire department. He said his life was a little chaotic at times, but they were making ends meet. Then came the question to me: "What do you do?"

I explained that, like Phil, I also had two jobs. My dilemma was which to share first. "I'm a part-time professor at a local college."

"Cool. What do you teach?"

"Human Sexuality—it's a psychology course," I responded.

"Wild. Now *that's* something you don't hear everyday! What else do you do?" Phil asked.

Now here's where I thought it'd get awkward, but I continued on. "Well, my main passion in life is helping people reconnect with God. The best way I've found to do that is to pastor a church."

After a chuckle, he asked what the church was called (probably expecting something like The Church of the Holy Virgins). Sheepishly, I said, "Vineyard Christian Fellowship."

Then the story took off. As it turned out, Phil's wife attended a Vineyard church in Colorado while they were dating and when they first married. It happened to be in the town where I grew up, and its pastor is one of my best friends. A connection was made. Phil went on to tell me how he had never been to a church, but his wife seemed to really like the music and stuff they did there. Since they'd been in Butte, she had been disconnected from the God stuff but periodically tried churches around the area. She really wanted him to go, but he wasn't sure what kept him away from the whole God thing.

God was knocking, and now Phil opened the door. "My wife will freak out when she hears I met a Vineyard pastor, especially one that teaches sex. Maybe God is trying to tell us something. Hey, do you want to go over and see the fire station I work at? It's right next door to the transmission shop we're taking your truck to."

Suddenly, my transmission problem seemed less problematic and more providential. God was at work in the lives of this young couple and knew it would take a somewhat nontraditional encounter with a follower of Christ to get their attention. Of course, I still prayed, "God, next time could you do it with just a flat tire or something?"

Look around your life. How many things occur in your week that just seem to be bad luck, good luck, or even coincidence? Is it possible that God may be trying to merge your life into the story he is writing?

GROWTH POINTS

1. There's a big difference between asking God to be a part of our story and our becoming a part of his. Ask Jesus to give you eyes to see something he is doing this week that you can be a part of. No matter how large or small it appears, commit to be obedient. You may have to step out of your routine.

2. Read Hebrews 11 and pick a couple of faith heroes that are listed there. Read their story in detail in the Old Testament (many Bibles show cross-references to Old Testament passages). Did they merge their lives into God's story, or did they ask God to become a part of theirs? Was the result always comfort and happiness?

More Than Rhetoric

Many of us have been taught to memorize Bible verses out of context and live by the warm fuzzy rhetoric of wall plaques for so long that we have lost our part in the larger story. In order for the kingdom of God to thrive in my life, I must be willing to *be* a part of it, not just *say* that I am.

For me, that means admitting that simply saying, "PBPGIFWMY" (Please be patient, God isn't finished with me yet) can't support the weight of most of the relationship turmoil I cause. I need to find God's redemptive story in those everyday relationships. I can do that if I understand that God has been writing a story from the beginning of time. Its central focus is Jesus and the divine community we call the Trinity. Its theme is the passionate pursuit of redemption of all God has created. God doesn't want me to be a religious pretender in everyday circumstances; he wants me to face life's challenges with a desire to see myself within the context of his larger story.

We have been asked to enter the story at *this time* and in *this place* to be the people he created us to be. Bible texts help us see the theme and purpose of the story and how to live within the parameters of the plot, but we must live out our part under the directorship of the Holy Spirit. He won't contradict his own story line, but he'll help us live in such a way that the plot builds to the ultimate crescendo we read about in the final act—the book of Revelation.

What will happen if we begin to walk around our towns and workplaces asking God to let us live his story today? Our faith will become something that we don't just add into our lives but something we actually live. We will begin to see everything around us as potentially God's script. Even the "bad" things that happen will give us the potential to improvise and bring about ultimate good and glory.

We will grow. We will grow in our understanding of how God's kingdom can affect our everyday lives and how our everyday lives can contribute to his kingdom. We will grow in depth in our relationship with Christ. We will grow through our relationships with others. We will leave the life of bonsai far behind, inspiring others to do the same.

Activity Versus Progress

The growth of God's kingdom in our lives is not some haphazard tourist trip in which Dad piles all the kids into the wood-paneled minivan with no map or destination—only a desire to drive and see where Route 24 actually goes. There is a goal, a final destination that we seek. In his letter to the Ephesians, the apostle Paul gave us a compass heading when he wrote,

> The body of Christ may be built up until we all reach
> unity in the faith and in the knowledge of the Son of
> God and become mature, attaining to the whole meas-
> ure of Christ's fullness.
> Then we will no longer be infants, tossed back and
> forth by the waves, and blown here and there by every
> wind of teaching and by the cunning and craftiness of
> men in their deceitful scheming. (Ephesians 4:12-14)

Paul's goal was for believers in Jesus to grow up and ultimately attain the whole measure of the fullness of Christ. Paul saw us as Jesus sees us—full of potential to flourish in our relationship with Christ and in our influence in the garden we live in. But there's a lot of time and sweat between being a little sprout and massive sequoia.

You and I can't just wish we were mature and expect it to

happen. If we do, we will find ourselves cruising the golden years wearing the diapers of infancy. So this change process must be planned and then empowered by Jesus, the Master of Life.

Still, planning alone doesn't guarantee success. We must also ensure that we are making progress, for perhaps second to laziness, busyness without progress sucks the potential right out of us and ultimately stunts our growth.

There's a fascinating story about one of the early North Pole explorers. He was disciplined enough to chart his journey hourly to ensure that he stayed on course through the white wasteland. At one point a strange phenomenon began. He would stop and check his position, and even though his instruments indicated that he had been moving northward, he was actually farther south than he had been at his last reading. Regardless of the speed at which he walked in what he thought was the Pole's direction, he continued to get farther and farther from it.

What bizarre situation had he stumbled upon? Were his instruments on the fritz? Was he somehow transported into an episode of *The X-Files?*

Finally, he discovered that he had ventured onto an enormous iceberg that was drifting in one direction as he was walking in the other.

What a profound lesson in this explorer's journey! We have to realize the subtle difference between activity and progress. Sure, this unfortunate explorer had planned to reach the North Pole, but he started his journey in a context that would actually pull him further from his goal than when he started. That is as true in our growth in a friendship with Jesus as it is on a North Pole expedition.

Ponder the things in your religious life that keep you busy but ultimately produce little or no progress. Are there some activities that may even be causing your walk with Jesus to go "south"?

From potluck dinners to Bible studies, sometimes our schedules are so full of Christian activities that we have no time for God. Our church lives become so full of words that we begin to drown in our own sea of Christianese and rhetoric. When was the last time you stopped your Bible study group and said, "Hold on. Let's review the past six months and honestly evaluate how we are living in the areas we have studied"?

Most of us are running Bible studies in turbo-charged, high-octane-fueled racing vehicles. We set our goal to read through the Bible in a year as if that were the checkered flag to maturity. The subtle goal is to get smarter and not necessarily transparent with the Word of God and each other. Thus, we begin to measure success by the activity and not the progress. In other words, we talk about growth and yet don't realize we are adrift on the larger iceberg of busyness and religiosity. The deeper question should be, *Am I more like my Master Jesus when it is over?*

The Christian life is meant to be one of growth and progress, while the bonsai life prefers empty busyness and distraction. The apostle Peter wrote, "But grow in the grace and knowledge of our Lord and Savior Jesus Christ" (2 Peter 3:18). How can we know that we are growing in grace, that we are making real progress and not merely deceiving ourselves with activity?

In my town, I drive half a mile to the health club, struggle to find a parking spot as close to the door as I can, and then work out for forty-five minutes before I start thinking about lunch. One of my favorite pieces of cardiovascular equipment is the StairMaster. This stationary machine simulates climbing stairs and automatically adjusts the speed and resistance of your climb according to the workout you choose. Sometimes it amazes me how I can work up a sweat, see my heart rate soar to 150 beats per minute, have the machine tell me I climbed the equivalent of two full miles, and then stop—getting off the machine in the very same place I started. That may be all right for exercise, but it's no way to travel!

It is much the same with our progress toward God. We must not only work hard at times to see progress but we must be sure we are progressing in the right areas. Many times, we convince ourselves that the activities we participate in are helping us climb higher and higher, when in reality, the best they might be doing is keeping us in the same place.

From Desire to Discipline to Delight

Given the years I've spent in health clubs, you would think I could body-double for Vin Diesel. Most who know me say I have a better shot doubling for Danny DeVito. But like many participants in the health-club industry, my discipline comes and goes, counter-cyclical to the holiday and fun seasons. I work out hard for a few months and then feast with family and friends from Thanksgiving through Super Bowl Sunday in January. Come February, I'm back at it with commitment and discipline till around May, when the Northwest weather turns sunny again. I get distracted with lawn care, playing at the beach with my family, and visits from out-of-state friends. The whole routine resembles the binge-and-purge Christianity we discussed earlier.

Does your walk with God tend to follow this pattern?

Take prayer, for example. Like me, you may have read many books challenging us to be people of prayer. I've heard countless teachings telling me how real men and women of God spend at least one hour every morning praying. I've heard and read so much that I can actually teach a pretty good series on prayer, even though my personal life doesn't reflect what I profess with my mouth. That makes me a perfect candidate for "Bonsai Prayer Warrior of the Year"!

But the truth is, just knowing my potential to engage in meaningful conversation with God is not enough. Oh, how much potential we have to grow and be fruitful in prayer and not just pretend it to be so! Too often, I've been content to profess one thing and experience another.

For some reason, I've always had the hardest time getting my body disciplined enough to rise early in the morning for a "quiet time." I've tried some of those fantastic prayer techniques: (1) start with just five minutes per day for the first week and then add five minutes each week thereafter, or (2) keep a prayer list of names and needs to help you focus, or (3) read more about great prayer people so you'll ultimately feel guilty enough to pray more yourself. (You know the tools and techniques of Christendom as well as I do.) For me, most of them only succeeded in making me busy so I appeared more credible in pretending I was a prayer warrior. What a shame that I never allowed them to actually bring me closer to God.

So why don't we change? Why do we put in all this effort and yet accomplish little long-term growth in our relationship with Jesus?

For me, the change in my prayer life came when I realized I was praying for all the wrong reasons. For years I struggled with prayer because I knew it was the "spiritual" thing to do. People I admired prayed, so I thought I should too. But in my core, it wasn't really to fall more in love with God; it was to look more mature. It wasn't because my soul knew I needed to; it was because my mind told me I should. I wanted others to think I was mature in prayer without actually having to be.

So I began praying for the desire to pray more. As the desire grew, I found that what I had seen as techniques and tools were actually disciplines. Thus, I had to ask Jesus to begin changing my burgeoning desire into a practice that worked for me. That discipline came as God began to show me the direct link between my prayer life and my wife and kids' spiritual well-being. When I began to let up, the enemy let in.

I'm nowhere near a prayer warrior like Hudson Taylor, Martin Luther, or Oswald Chambers, but spending time with Jesus has begun to be a truly tangible experience. It hasn't happened overnight, but desire has moved to discipline, and discipline is changing to delight. I realize that just believing in the power of prayer is not enough. My life needs to merge with my beliefs if I am going to experience true vitality in my prayer life.

It helps knowing that the same empowering presence of the Holy Spirit resides within me as it did with those other bona fide conversationalists. That gives me the hope that indeed I am a plant with a lot of growth potential. If I can grow in prayer, I'm sure I can do it in other areas as well. Maybe I'll ask God to unleash compassion or healing in me next. Who knows?

Whatever area he targets, I know I can't do it alone. I need partners who are also collaborating with Jesus.

GROWTH POINTS

1. If you're a notetaker, you'll like this. Review your collection of Bible-study notes over the past year or so. How big is the gap between what you have learned and who you are in your daily living? Why does that gap exist?

2. Make a list of spiritual disciplines you participate in during the week, such as prayer, Bible reading, or church attendance. Is each one adding substance to your intimacy with Jesus, or just helping you maintain a facade? Are they more for activity, or progress? If you see a problem, is it the tool, or the way you're using it?

CHAPTER 3

EMBRACE THE POWER OF COMMUNITY

IT MAKES NO SENSE to have a plant with lots of potential and then squeeze it into a restrictive container—unless your goal is to grow a bonsai tree.

According to convention, the ratio should be 80 percent bonsai plant to 20 percent container. The diminutive pot makes the tree look bigger than it is. The container should look good but not detract from the plant's beauty by being too gaudy or mundane. When the tree is standing alone, it's important that the viewer's perception be manipulated.

Also, the pot needs to be shallow so the roots can't reach very deep. The container gives only enough support for the tree to survive, not thrive. This way, the tree doesn't grow to its potential and doesn't need to be replanted into a new container.

Just as the wrong container can stunt a plant's growth, the right container can help a plant reach its fullest potential. When we think about the container we grow in as Christians, the picture that most readily comes to mind is a church building. But that's only a small piece of the story. The strongest enhancers and constrictors of growth are the relationships we choose—inside and outside of those brick-and-mortar chapels. Traditions, bylaws, and unwritten expectations that accompany those relationships also affect our growth.

The writer of Hebrews tells us that in order to pursue a true friendship with Christ, we must "consider how we may spur one another on toward love and good deeds. Let us not give up meeting together, as some are in the habit of doing, but let us encourage one another—and all the more as you see the Day approaching" (Hebrews 10:24-25). A psalmist wrote, "Planted in the house of the LORD, they shall flourish in the courts of our God" (Psalm 92:13).

It's not my duty to judge the pots that others are thriving or dying in. I am, however, responsible to examine the container in which I am growing. Personally, I thrive in a church environment where there are few rules and chaos seems more the norm than reverence. I once had a pastor ask me if a certain young man who had been visiting his church had come from mine. I asked him how he had come to that conclusion. He replied, "Yours is the only church I know of where someone would feel free enough to break-dance during worship!"

Others come into my church and feel distracted, underpierced, or even offended by the diversity of tattoos showcased on body parts. That type of person may thrive in a more traditional church setting, where structure and protocol keep people focused and in line. It is my job not to judge the container but to help people find the right container that will foster the fullest potential growth in their relationship with Christ.

The Power of Community

Our need for community is more and more obvious today. The breakdown of the traditional family and the desire to be part of something greater than ourselves are motivating many disciples to get reconnected. We're remembering that God himself is the ultimate three-in-one community: Father, Son, and Holy Spirit. Many of us have been following the bonsai way by default simply by settling for community life that is small and shallow. But all over our culture, shallow pots are beginning to shatter against the Rock.

For some, coffee is coffee, but for the committed, Starbucks is *not* Folgers. The same seems true for this emerging generation and its attitude toward community. Something new is brewing. This generation seems to have an uncanny ability to seek God in traditional brick-and-mortar houses of God without falling into their associated bureaucracies. Couple that trend with the view that spirituality is a journey and not necessarily a destination, and we have something that looks like bricks with wings.

Historically, the search for God has fallen into one of two camps: *institutions* or *journeys*. The institutional paradigm sees God as existing in a place. The place where God dwells thus becomes holy. Whether in a monastic community with its cool, damp stone walls of the fifth century, the great Gothic cathedrals of the eleventh century, or the shining purple-and-gold TBN stage set in modern America, institutionalists know God can be found under their roof. We draw boundaries around these places, call them sacred, and protect them.

Humans innately need a tangible place to find God. Even Hollywood echoes this theme: When characters need to pray or find refuge, they usually end up within the walls of a traditional church building. These permanent structures feel secure and stable.

But more common are those who hold images of sacred journeys rather than of dwelling places. Spirituality is portable, not permanent; malleable, not stable; mysterious and uncontainable, not placed in holy and tangible structures. The line between the sacred and the profane becomes blurred.

We have birthed a generation of wanderers. We seek places to settle but still desire faith to be a journey. We seek a God who is stable but not dogmatic. We are returning to ritual and tradition while holding to the values of diversity and change.

Is it possible to have bricks with wings? Yes, if you call it *community*. Neither mortar and stone nor bylaws and bureaucracy can bind this new community. It's a place where people can find stability, tradition, and permanence while maintaining freedom to explore and follow the guidance of Jesus.

Many have shunned the manufactured, bylaw-driven, cookie-cutter model of church life that turned out to be like a Hollywood stage prop—very real until someone leaned on it too hard for support. We long for stable community, not a bonsai community of bonsai believers. Healthy community breeds healthy followers of Christ.

Choose Your Pot Wisely

The size of the pot can greatly affect the mass and health of a tree. Bonsai believers pot themselves in small, shallow, and often pretty pots because that's what helps them look best. But believers who want real growth need deep pots. Brick or shantytown, house church or crystal cathedral—neither the size of the building nor the size of the congregation matters. What creates the right container is the vastness and depth of the people's spirituality and vision.

Believers who want to grow healthy and bear much fruit would do well to study St. David of Pembrokeshire, the sixth-century saint who helped plant Christian faith in Wales. He understood the ancient truth that healthy community produces healthy followers.

When the Roman armies left England early in the fifth century, they took not only their military might and money but also the traditions and structure of the Christian faith, creating a vast cultural and religious vacuum. Not long after, the Celtic people were pushed westward and north by the Anglo-Saxon invasion. Life was disrupted, routines shaken, and families separated.

People had to fend for themselves. Among the Celts, certain small groups banded together to keep their Christian faith pure and strong. These little bands grew into flourishing monastic communities. Today, many emerging church leaders look to the Celtic communities as sources of inspiration and guidance as they try to navigate a new culture in which Christianity seems to have been relegated to the corners of society.

St. David's story begins with a monk named Illtyd, who started a monastic community that emphasized discovering one's calling and being trained to fulfill it. One of those Illtyd trained was David, son of Non. David was raised knowing the importance of faith and is said to have memorized the entire book of Psalms.

David felt God's call to gather souls "together in bundles" (see Matthew 9:37-38). He spent years learning at various monastic communities. In time, the Holy Spirit led David and three of his companions to build an extensive mission center in Pembrokeshire, David's birthplace.

David was ordained a bishop in AD 540 and died almost fifty years later. During those years, he helped develop a remarkable community of people. Individuals would travel to his community, learn and grow in the ways of the Lord, and then go out as missionaries to Wales, England, and Scotland. David was not an overly charismatic leader. Instead, he relied heavily on the power of community and the leading of God to change lives. David was willing to get his hands dirty with those he mentored. He worked alongside them and shared life with them. He didn't just give them books to read on ministry; he ministered with them.

When we think of mentoring or discipleship today, we often imagine downloading information into someone's head, not living a transparent lifestyle with someone. For David, community and mentoring were about a shared lifestyle. He was incredibly strict by today's religious powder-puff community standards. But he partook in whatever he dished out.

When not at prayer or in services, David and the monks spent their time working hard on the land. They used the fruits of their labor to feed the needy. David impressed upon his followers that ministering to the poor was central for a follower of Christ. Side by side they tilled the land, without horses or cattle, pushing plows with their bare hands. The container for growth that David's community provided was holistic—it touched the soul, the spirit, and the flesh of everyone around them.[1]

I often dream about the opportunity to travel back in time and experience such a community. I believe to walk behind those plows and listen in on those prayers would cure my sentimentality about what it means to have a kingdom-oriented community. But because I can't travel back in time, I have done the next best thing. I've traveled east to a Christian community that really works: The Church of the Saviour in the Adams Morgan district of Washington DC. It's close to a twenty-first-century version of what I imagine David's sixth-century community to have been. The members of the Church of the Savior pursue both the inward journey of faith and the outward journey of social justice. Gordon Cosby and his wife, Mary, lead this community to find the substance of their lives in pursuing Christ and ministering to the broken in their neighborhood. When someone in the church senses a call from God for service, the church prays about it, and if God is in it, the vision is refined and a handful of members commit to bringing it to fruition.

Over a cup of soup at the Potter's House, a coffeehouse run by the church, eighty-plus-year-old Gordon shared with me how much more can be accomplished by ten people who discover and live within their call than one hundred who are unsure. His desire is to lead people to living from the focused center of God's kingdom and then following the call God gives them. When I asked him why more churches don't follow his example and better their cities, he responded with a rather sobering comment: "Because the servant leadership Jesus offers us is a leadership toward unimpressiveness."

David and Gordon have made "bricks with wings." By contrast, some Christian communities are like the Borg species in *Star Trek: The Next Generation,* whose goal is to assimilate as many people as possible, stealing their individuality in order to enhance the collective's power. But in their different ways, David and Gordon developed places where people could mature in their calling without becoming ingrown and isolated. David's monastery was merely a stop on people's spiritual pilgrimages toward God's calling. Gordon's community is simply a place to discover God's call on their lives that could change someone's world. Both have provided places of transition in which people get locked not into titles but into a life orientation toward Christ. Both have ensured that people grow in containers larger than what David or Gordon by themselves could envision.

God Builds the Pot

So how do these perspectives help us build nonrestrictive but life-giving pots today? First, God has been in the business of transforming lives through the church since the story of Acts unfolded. How effectively we have allowed the Holy Spirit to be in that process has ebbed and flowed throughout history. Today's healthiest churches are no longer measuring success by the ABCs (Attendance, Buildings, and Checkbooks) but by their ability to produce genuine followers of Christ.

Life-giving community breeds life-giving followers; bonsai communities breed bonsai followers. That's why the container we're growing in is so crucial. Shallow pots produce shallow roots, which generate shallow people with shallow spirituality.

What makes a community life-giving in today's climate of relativism, compromise, and candy-coated Sunday programs? Do we all need to live in monasteries like St. David's or in the inner city like Church of the Savior? No. To do so would be to gather around the effect of what they have done and miss the core that caused it. We have to take the time to grow deeper and pursue Jesus until he reveals our callings, both as individuals and as communities.

Over a cup of java, I'm sure we could generate an entire checklist of features that are more likely than not to foster life and depth in a community. But just checking requirements off a list isn't the key, as that would at best turn us into cookie-cutter churches and at worst make us legalistic, pharisaical communities. Still, just a cursory reading of the New Testament shows that the early churches had a way of allowing the Holy Spirit to spend them on the horizontal, by serving and loving, while simultaneously having their own lives transformed on the vertical, through worship and study. That's the way of the Cross: to go and make disciples while we continue to apprentice ourselves to the Master Jesus.

GROWTH POINTS

1. How do you see your search for God? Are you drawn to a place/building, or a journey? What could you learn from experiencing the other?

2. How would you assess whether a church is "healthy"? Do the "ABCs" mentioned earlier have any legitimacy?

The Power of Culture

Not only do the people we hang out with influence the depth and breadth of our pot but so does the larger context of the culture in which we live. Like gravity, it is an unseen and often taken-for-granted force that influences everything around us. Push on its boundaries and you realize it's there. Depending on your approach, denying it altogether will either set you free or cause you a world of hurt. That's how culture works; it shapes our lives and filters our view. It is not, however, indomitable.

We are often unaware how the culturally filtered information we receive changes the way we see the world around us. Culture colors the lenses through which every generation views community. For our generation, the colors come from science, business management, psychotherapy, and good ol' cable television. We need to honestly evaluate the ways in which these models do or don't enhance the kind of communities that foster spiritual health.

Grab your mental remote and click back to the early 1990s' TV talk show heyday. We were led down the inspirational path of deeper understanding of the human psyche by television gurus like Oprah Winfrey, Ricki Lake, Montel Williams, and Phil Donahue. For a period of time, it appeared that the theme of the season was adopted children being reunited with their biological mothers and fathers.

Cameras zoomed in on the apprehensive, teary-eyed faces of thirty-year-old children as they waited for their long lost biological mothers to exit the walkway tunnel of the airplane. Would they embrace? Would they be able to say, "I love you"? Americans were mesmerized by the excitement and potential healing that accompanied these events. But in the background of our culture, another strange phenomenon was occurring.

While America watched these joyous reunions and sometimes painful rejections, adoption agencies were beginning to experience a chill. They saw a dramatic decline in the number of women who were willing to consider adoption as an option for an unwanted pregnancy. More and more young women feared that their child would someday show up on their doorstep expecting a hug and a place to live. The present angst of pregnancy was enough to go through without having to consider future relationship repercussions. Many opted out of the pregnancy altogether, and the abortion rate continued to rise.[2]

Filtered information influenced the way we, as a culture, responded to pregnancies. Many felt it was almost inevitable that children of adoption would one day seek reunions. In reality, fewer than five percent of all adopted children ever try to find their biological parents.[3] Nonetheless, our worldview was tainted.

What could you be viewing today that is tainting your tomorrow?

I started my church at the age of thirty, a card-carrying member of Generation X. I could see that my generation and the millennials after us had been raised in a world that blended big chunks of the modernist mindset, the values of our boomer parents, and a hint of the silent generation. We were wearing some funky-colored lenses when it came to viewing community, and I was convinced that today's church needed more edge to reach a swiftly changing culture. Now eight years later, I'm figuring out that the problem isn't *them* (Christians older than I am), because we're all in this together. And now I'm realizing that my community needs more prayer to sharpen that edge I'm so proud of. No doubt in the next eight years

I'll have another brilliant insight that somebody thought of fifteen centuries ago.

My point is, we must be careful not to assume that we have finally figured out what community is about. Yet at the same time we must be willing to make some tracks in seemingly uncharted territory. The question is, *Are we willing to break the bonsai-driven molds of church containers when we see them?*

More Than CEOs and Therapists

The church has often shaped its view of what community is while wearing cultural goggles. The Puritans saw the church and government as inextricably linked, while the Anabaptists sought to withdraw from society and political rule and return to primitive Christianity. Modernism awoke in the seventeenth century's scientific revolution and produced a view of church community that sought to compete with science. Three centuries later, still riding that wave, evangelical children of the 1970s cut their teeth on Josh McDowell's *Evidence That Demands a Verdict* and countless creation-versus-evolution seminars. Not to be outdone, the 1990s ushered in the era of churches being seeker-sensitive and techno-savvy.

My generation, Gen X, has also grown up in a church culture in which community is predominately seen through the lenses of the CEO and the therapist. We have been taught that healthy churches are run like businesses that aim to make people feel good about themselves and God. Vision building, knowing your target market, and working the budget to maximize output have dominated most church leadership training circles. Sadly, sometimes the technique takes precedence over the purpose. Still we spend an immense amount of energy and money on perpetuating the ideals, because that is the pot we are trying to grow in.

Perhaps something in you has been screaming that the church is more than just an organization. You can feel the roots of your relationship with God pushing against the sides of a container that is supposed to be helping you grow. You know the church is a life, a body, an entity that cannot, and will not, succumb to the constricting paradigms of the day. Perhaps that's why in the Bible, God used so many metaphors to describe his people. In that way, we'd be less likely to force community to fit into just one neat and tidy little box. The New Testament is full of pictures of what community is like:

A BODY:
"The body is a unit, though it is made up of many parts; and though all its parts are many, they form one body. So it is with Christ" (1 Corinthians 12:12). This metaphor has helped us learn to value everyone's gifts and contribution in the church and recognize Jesus as the true leader of the "one holy church."

A TEMPLE:
"In him the whole building is joined together and rises to become a holy temple in the Lord" (Ephesians 2:21). The typology of the Old Testament temple has fostered a sense of holiness and reverence for God's presence in our midst.

A FLOCK OF SHEEP:
"May the God of peace, who through the blood of the eternal covenant brought back from the dead our Lord Jesus, that great Shepherd of the sheep. . ." (Hebrews 13:20). So many paintings, so many shepherd sermons, and so many illustrations have helped us understand

the gentleness, compassion, and protection of Jesus for his flock.

A FAMILY:

"How great is the love the Father has lavished on us, that we should be called children of God! And that is what we are!" (1 John 3:1). If we didn't know God as a loving father and his people as a family, God's discipline would appear tyrannical and abusive and our relationships with others disconnected.

A FARM FIELD:

"For we are God's fellow workers; you are God's field" (1 Corinthians 3:9). Knowing we are a field helps us understand and press through the seasons of life with others.

A BRIDE:

"Let us rejoice and be glad and give him glory! For the wedding of the Lamb has come, and his bride has made herself ready" (Revelation 19:7). Perhaps no metaphor better stresses the intimate and personal nature of the reciprocal love God desires with us.

Please don't just skim over these verses. Each has a purpose, or else the Holy Spirit wouldn't have written it in his book. But what would happen if the church, your church for instance, insisted on just one? Or to a lesser degree, what happens when the emphasis is predominately just one? Isn't it possible that we could begin to make the metaphor more important than its inherent purpose or intent?

I assert that the church has often tried to force God to fit into

its metaphor of the day versus seeing a metaphor for what it is—
just a metaphor.

Regardless of the picture, one thing remains consistent throughout the Word of God regarding church community: Jesus Christ is
the center, not us. It is Jesus who is the head, Jesus who is the
source of life, Jesus who is the cornerstone, Jesus who is the groom.

Throw Away the Box

Thus, perhaps the best way to think outside the box when it comes
to finding community is to throw the box away altogether and use the
Book instead. The gigantic trees that grow by the river of life are held
in a container no smaller than the earth itself. So let's not try to force
the church into any metaphor but instead use metaphors to help us
understand the church. Jesus is the Master of his church. He knows
what life-giving community looks like in any culture and for any age
group. He knows what his community should look like in your city
and mine. He used metaphors and parables to help us understand
him and the nature of his kingdom, not so he could understand us.

I have a friend in Idaho who pastors a church that meets in a
barn. Seems that when he started asking Jesus to show him what
type of church to build, Jesus responded with a vision and voice
that would make even Wyatt Earp and Billy the Kid take notice. A
church in a barn—craziest thing I've ever seen. I'm sure couples
argue on their way to church like most every churchgoing family
does, but that's where the similarities end.

His service starts late in the morning so all the folks have time
to get their ranching chores done. The entire lower level of the
church structure is full of horse stalls and a couple of tack rooms.
If you want to participate in worship in this sanctuary, you've got
to walk through the barn doors, step over any cow pies, and find

the steps that climb up to the hay-filled floors of this cowboy church. The upper deck of this barn consists of a big room with a wood stove on each side and seating for about eighty people. Kids and adults worship with a country twang and hear the Word of God together as one big family.

It's a cowboy community church for a bunch of cowboys. Something tells me that when it comes to understanding flocks and fields in the Bible, these guys and gals could hang their hats on it. It is a place that resonates with who they are and allows the presence of God to move in their midst. They are developing a pot that is bigger and wider and deeper than many of them have ever known. I'm sure my cowboy friend is glad he listened to the Master Jesus.

The point is, if we choose to bow to Jesus' leadership and not the metaphor of the day, if we commit to following his lead and not the systematic book approach du jour, if we focus on his community with Father and Spirit and not the pseudo-communities offered by the world, we might *actually become* a group that overflows with health and life.

GROWTH POINTS

1. The Bible is one of the most picturesque and metaphorical books ever written. Page through a concordance and find some metaphors for God's people. Write them down and provide any examples from your experiences.

2. What is the dominant metaphor in your current faith community? Can you substantiate it biblically? How has this model helped you grow toward the community Jesus wants you to be, and how has it hindered it?

Same Dance, New Rhythm

Our growth toward a cooperative friendship with Jesus requires constant reevaluation and redefinition. It's not a static state but a fluid relationship between the Master and us. While the dance of spiritual growth remains consistent in many ways throughout the centuries, each generation and each faith community needs to find its own rhythm. A gift Gen Xers have is that we aren't afraid to take the gospel to the streets and shelters of our culture, and we have developed a higher value for connection and a lower value on hierarchy.

I remember in middle school attending my first dance. What an overwhelming event for a short kid just hitting puberty! Our immense cafeteria, which normally had mustard stains on the walls and last week's Jell-O remnants stuck under the tables, became a scene out of Soul Train. It was transformed with streamers, disco lighting, a thousand watts of hi-fi power, and a magical mirror ball that lured us into a Bee Gees–driven hypnotic state. We boys stood on one side of the room, hands in our pockets, putting on our most confident look. The girls stood on the other side of the vast dance floor, giggling and talking about who knows what. The night was young and I was petrified, but the music played on.

That was my first dancing experience. As time went on, I had many opportunities to redefine what dancing encompassed. I gleaned dance experiences from the high school scene, groovin' at nightclubs, and participating in modern jazz choreography. Just when I thought I had it all figured out, I was introduced to the First Nations movement. I was taught to embrace the movements of different cultures, such as the powerful warrior dance of the Maori culture and the softer storytelling style of the Samoans.

Dance encompasses so much. Each form carries a unique expression of this universal rhythm of humanity. Pursuing a no-holds-barred relationship with Christ is like going dancing. As my relationship develops, I discover more and more about how to have a vibrant relationship with God and others. Our dance partner hasn't changed since the beginning of time, but the rhythms sure have.

We are called to move in harmony with Jesus' kingdom and keep in step with him. But often when I visit other churches, I feel like a punk rocker in a Lawrence Welk rerun. I try to fit in, but every rhythm I hear seems different from theirs. We all smile pleasantly at each other, but our discomfort with each other's style seems to drown out whatever music the Holy Spirit is playing. I'm glad they're enjoying the music and the bubbles, but my feet want to tangle instead of tango.

Still, we have to learn to honor each generation's rhythm. Once, I was visiting a wonderful traditional mainline church. Gerta, the organist, had me frantically finding hymn #272 while everyone else began to sing from memory. My ears cringed and felt like they were going to start bleeding as the old man behind me bellowed out the words: "Oh, what a friend we have in Jesus. All our sins and burdens to bear. . . . " (something like that).

To add to the pain, his wife had this incredible ability to be just half a word behind the entire congregation as she hollered the chorus. As I nervously paged through the hymnal, I hoped that some bouncer with a big hooked staff would quietly usher these two to the soundproof booth out back. Then it happened: A hand reached over my shoulder and gave me a hymnal opened to the page I was seeking and then gently withdrew. Now was my chance to see what form of humanity was screeching such horrid sounds. I turned to give a courteous thank-you and sneak a peek.

As my head turned around, my heart hit the worn wooden floor. What I saw was an elderly couple, faces weathered from life and eyes streaming with tears of love for "this friend they have in

Jesus." There was so much love oozing from them that their voices suddenly didn't sound horrid but heavenly. They were singing the song in perfect rhythm to their lives, and Jesus was pleased.

So it's not about judging the music but recognizing that we have our own dance to do. For followers of Christ, life is the ultimate dance and Jesus always leads. Genuine community to me is one with a rhythm to which I can move naturally.

Visiting churches of this generation, I've experienced a number of things that resonate with genuine community. The rhythm is changing. Some want to hold to the rerun of music gone by, which has its place. But others seek a new beat. And many on both sides of this disagreement live from a perspective that if something is different from what we like, it must be wrong. Different can be just different. Different can also mean progress—or regress—depending not on our preferences but on what God is up to. So every tradition must learn to seek God in the differences we encounter.

To those who dance to a different beat from what you may be hearing today: Please consider that just because it isn't your vibe, if you feel your toes getting stepped on these days, it may be that you are the one out of step with Jesus. He might want to expand your repertoire and teach you a new tune.

The Need for Leaders Who Nurture, Not Just Manage

Gen Xers see the church as more of a garden than a machine. Our goal is no longer just to grow numerically or profitably as a church but to nurture people individually within the context of our tribal community. Thus, today's leaders act more as fertilizers than managers.

Jesus set this example in Matthew 9:35–10:2 when he called his disciples (his community) together. Notice the change in terms for these followers of Jesus: "He called his twelve *disciples* to him and gave them authority to drive out evil spirits and to heal every disease and sickness. These are the names of the twelve *apostles* . . . " (Matthew 10:1-2, emphasis added).

A disciple in biblical times was an apprentice—someone who was dedicated to learning from a master. The apostles (literally, "sent ones") were sent out to do what the master did: build the kingdom of God by planting churches and providing leadership. These men were transformed from learners to doers. In a similar way, the body of Christ needs us to grow through community and develop leaders who don't just manage but mobilize, empower, and release others into kingdom living.

Latchkey Kids with an Attitude

Though some may be lamenting the glory days gone by, others are recognizing the credibility and potential of the latest Christ followers. Many have already developed some of the survival skills necessary to succeed in this new milieu, especially those raised as latchkey kids, forced by circumstances to fend for themselves and make the best of their days.

I spent the formative years of my life on the front porch of my home, cared for by a brother only two years older than I. Neglect was the fruit of a home where my biological mom suffered from depression and my dad spent many a long day making ends meet. After their eventual divorce, God redeemed my early days when my father married a different woman who truly became a mother of presence and sound mind. My story is not unique; many of these makers of new community come from single-parent households, homes where addiction was more prominent than affection, or lives where the streets or a car were the only home they knew for a season.

Regardless of the specifics, adversity and affliction not only produce pain but they can also generate toughness and resilience. This new breed of Christian community isn't as concerned about acceptance from without but knows the importance of acceptance from within their tribe. They value bonding together, sharing together, and developing skills to survive a world that is trying to ignore them. They tend to be unruly, rough around the edges, and less concerned about boards and committees than about warfare and worship. Their bodies are pierced and they color their skin, sometimes to express shared pain and tribalism.

Connectivity Is "Connect with Me"

Many of today's emergent churches have flat organizational charts rather than traditional, pyramid-shaped systems with centralized power. Influence comes from honest relationship. Bridges of genuine trust and love between people bear the weight of confrontation. Positional authority doesn't mean much, but relational authority does. Once we have built significant, trusting relationships, we will find a way to survive whatever schemes this millennium holds.

Moving with today's rhythm, faith is not necessarily taught from the top down but from within our relational communities. Thus, for more and more people, relational community that produces life-giving faith is less about big productions and more about day-to-day relationships. Two hours with you, Jesus, java, and a bagel may produce more fruit in my life than attending four information-laden conferences focused on "living the Christian life." How ironic that those big conferences can produce such small containers to grow in while small, honest relationships can produce such spacious soil.

Case in point: When I was a teen, I remember sitting in a coliseum full of other youth and motivated parents listening to hour upon hour of seminars designed to solve every problem I would encounter. The lectures and accompanying big red book made submission to authority, morality, and adolescent stress so neat and tidy. But I work with kids who have been raped by their fathers, introduced to ecstasy drugs at age nine, and bounced in and out of foster care for six years. I can't find the chapter on how to help them wrestle with homosexual feelings and hatred toward the opposite sex in my big red book, but there's a grandmother in my church who can explain it.

She helps the world make sense to teen girls while teaching them to bake cookies and knead bread dough. These young girls share their lives with her in the presence of love, not laws. They become transparent in the shadow of nurture, not the spotlight of legalism.

I'm sure that seminar ministry has helped countless kids, but when we allow institutionalism to replace community, the safety of a grandma's arms, and the wisdom of her experiences, we've got a problem. Learning may occur at both the corporate and relational levels, but life happens at its best down here.

Even the power and excitement of Pentecost occurred more on a relational level than a corporate one. When it began, Jesus' disciples "were all together in one place" (Acts 2:1). After the big event, the power bore fruit in the soil of community. The believers prayed together, stayed together, ate together, learned together, and even survived financially together:

> All the believers were together and had everything in
> common. Selling their possessions and goods, they
> gave to anyone as he had need. Every day they contin-
> ued to meet together in the temple courts. They broke
> bread in their homes and ate together with glad and
> sincere hearts. (Acts 2:44-47)

Was one reason for all this togetherness survival? Maybe, like us, when they chose to identify with Christ, they not only were made new creations but also were even more marginalized in a culture that had just crucified the man they proclaimed as Lord.

Living on the margins of society, they found themselves over-taxed, disrespected, and often disemboweled. They needed each other's support just to survive. Yet this was the group the Holy Spirit wanted to use to change the world! They needed each other for encouragement, physical needs, and prayer. They were becoming the hand of Jesus to each other and to the streets around them.

Perhaps part of our problem is we see the power of Pentecost through the eyes of our incessant need for entertainment and idol worship. We love to showcase those who profess the mighty works of God. We shine a spotlight on them and then learn to live vicariously through their experiences.

What if the gifts of Pentecost were not for the stage but for the street? What if the real miracle of Pentecost was not that the disciples spoke in tongues but that God used them to speak the language of every culture within earshot?

More frequently, we are using our survival skills to overcome physical obstacles and stay focused on pursuing God's kingdom. Building the organizational structure of church is less appealing than building the organic connections of the body. We are drawn to community in small bands of believers who share our lives intimately and purposefully. As the rhythm of our culture changes, I hear the beat of the ancient church pounding louder and louder in my psyche.

Speaking of rhythm, I've heard that even plants respond to music and sounds. Some music helps them flourish, while other tunes cause them to wither. The rhythm of community has a big influence on whether I flourish in my relationship with Jesus or simply become satisfied with the inconsequentiality of a relationship that could be but really isn't.

GROWTH POINTS

1. Make a list of the top five reasons you attend the church that you do. How many (if any) reasons facilitate your experiencing the presence of Jesus? If you chose to, could you find the presence of God in each of your five reasons?

2. How have your life experiences and the generation you are from influenced your view of what Christian community is? What would you change if you could about how you live in community today?

3. Ponder community with Jesus this week. Ask him to speak to you through the culture, through his Word, and through his voice. What would he have you do with what he shared?

CHAPTER 4

ENRICH YOUR SOIL

HAVE YOU SEEN THOSE Miracle-Gro commercials suggesting that just a small treatment of fertilizer will turn your tomatoes into bowling-ball-size behemoths?

Miracle-Gro is a definite no-no in Bonsaiville. The key is not to put much fertilizer in the soil because fertilizer encourages roots to grow. Fertilizer also encourages healthier, larger, and sweeter fruit. Instead, it's imperative to make sure the soil encourages the water to run off and doesn't let the roots soak. Of course, as with all aspects of bonsai horticulture, the soil must *look* rich, dark, and full of life while actually containing only very little substance.

Proper nutrition helps the cells of our body grow strong. They communicate with each other clearly and fend off sickness effectively. Likewise, to grow as followers of Christ, we must find the source of proper nutrition. We need a source rich in nutrients and endless in supply. In biblical terms,

> "Man does not live on bread alone, but on every word
> that comes from the mouth of God." (Matthew 4:4)

Like newborn babies, crave pure spiritual milk, so that
by it you may grow. (1 Peter 2:2)

Why is it so easy to pick up almost any reading material other
than the Bible? Some would rather read a mystery novel, when the
Bible contains the greatest mystery ever revealed. Some would
rather read a romance, when the Bible is the greatest love story
ever told. Some turn to tabloids and sleaze, yet the Bible contains
some great trashy scenarios (like David and Bathsheba or Sampson
and Delilah) with redeeming insight.

Perhaps we have been convinced that the Bible is too compli-
cated for those without seminary training. Perhaps we really don't
believe what we read on its pages and, thus, would rather take it
apart than take it to heart.

I don't know everyone's reasons for not disciplining his or her
life in the Word of God (mine change almost seasonally), but I do
know that staying in the Word of God will keep the soil of your
heart tilled, fresh, and fertilized. Ask the Author himself to guide
you as you read his book. You will soon find that the Bible is the
only book in the world that you don't read but rather it reads you.

Fertilizer Stealers

One reason we have God's message in print is to continually
infuse life into heart soil that easily goes barren. Vitality doesn't
just happen to us; it must be pursued tenaciously and consistently.
Our culture almost imperceptibly steals vital nutrients from our
hearts and minds. Instead of a life wholly oriented toward Christ,
our culture urges an all-inclusive religious buffet. We're trying to
follow Jesus in a world where opposites can exist in the same
space:

- People yearn to get back to nature, but insist on doing it in high-tech $50,000 SUVs with built-in GPS systems and a cell phone.
- Families are getting smaller yet demanding larger homes in the suburbs to keep their ever-increasing material possessions.
- There is a dramatic rise in spirituality but less interest in traditional religion.
- We push the message of tolerance for all people, unless they happen to disagree with us.
- We demand solutions for children's violence yet keep the TV on for an average of seven hours a day. By the time a child leaves elementary school he or she has witnessed eight thousand murders.

But even in the midst of moral relativism and contradiction, a glimmer of hope shines. More and more pursuers of Christ are abandoning the marketing approach used by many churches in favor of something more genuine. Still, the soil we're starting with is in some ways more barren than in times past.

Have you ever asked someone if he believed in God? Historically, such a question meant, *Do you* trust *in God? Do you* believe *he is able to intervene in your circumstances today?* But as Western culture has drifted toward spiritual anarchy, we now ask the same question from an entirely different starting point. When I ask someone, "Do you believe in God?" I no longer assume the person has a basic belief that God exists. On one hand, we have an increase in spirituality, and on the other hand, the existence of God means a range of things to people. Some insightful people, like Kevin Hasson of the Becket Fund, have noted a strange dichotomy. Columnist George F. Will writes:

On one side, Hasson says, are those who believe that human beings have a natural thirst for transcendence, a built-in desire to live in communities enriched by rituals that express and slake that thirst. In the argot of the day, human beings are hardwired with religious sensibilities. On the other side are those who believe that the religious impulse is a bad habit, a legacy of less enlightened times, and something that society should outgrow. Religion is akin to secondhand smoke—something that thoroughly enlightened, modern people find obnoxious, and from which the public must be protected.[1]

I like the way Todd Hunter of Allelon Church Planting Foundation explains this new world: "We simply need to recognize the water that we are swimming in is different today." Changing times, changing culture—I don't think this confuses Jesus. After all, he is the Alpha and Omega, the beginning and the end. I don't see him up in heaven shaking his head wondering how to enrich the soil of our changing culture. Indeed, we can rest assured he has this and every emerging fading cultural mileu pretty well understood.

We live in a culture that appears to be becoming more spiritual while it simultaneously moves further away from genuine relationship with Christ. Defining exactly what has caused this "drying of the soil" is like attempting to nail Jell-O art to your living room wall. It can be frustrating and often fruitless. Still, there are some important arid patches to watch out for. Let's explore some things that can taint our soil and see if there are ways to overcome and even work within them.

Defining God

Growing in faith today challenges us to struggle with the notion of truth. Most of us are familiar with Jesus' statement "I am the way and the truth and the life" (John 14:6). Still, our new generation's soul wonders, *What do you mean, you are the "truth"?* Our culture once taught us that there was such a thing as "truth." It was definable, attainable, and reliable. The tenets of truth were as solid as a marble statue, having been chiseled throughout the ages out of the mountain of our unknowing. Church tradition and scholarship joined science on this bandwagon.

Christians built an entire monolithic structure called *systematic theology* on which to lay our belief. Incredibly, we found a way in our human understanding to identify, define, and document practically every concept that made up the Christian faith. Like laying the railroad ties and rails for a steam-driven locomotive, we kept putting one more theory or definition in front of the other, with few people stopping to ask, "Where is this train headed anyway?"

Have you ever paged through the church section in your city's yellow pages and counted the number of churches? For a real kick, compare that number to the number of pizza joints in your city. What does that tell you? In the 1800s, America had about thirty-six religious denominations. By Y2K, we found ourselves with more than four hundred denominations. Could it be that this great structure of theology was not only helping us define who we were but, more often, *who we were not?* We had schism after schism, church split after church split. Perhaps in our intellectual fervor to dissect the Word of God and elevate tradition, we were stealing the life-giving nutrients right out of God's Word and denying it to those who needed it. So the mystery of faith became not so much *Who is God, and how can I find him?* but more *Who knows God, and how do they* define *him?* Everybody fought to be the one authoritative voice that defined God and truth for everybody else.

In reaction against this fight, some have declared a cease-fire that doesn't get us any closer to a meaningful relationship with Christ. Truth and God are whatever an individual defines them to be. Truth isn't some solid marble statue, but more like the multi-colored ball of Play-Doh that I can squeeze into any shape I desire.

When I was a kid, my Play-Doh always started in its own color-coordinated container, but over time the dough mixed and I found myself working with an eclectic version of what used to be pure. That's not much different from how many see truth today. We've played with it enough that though its substance still seems visible, it sure has taken on a different color, shape, and (dare I say) flavor.

Do you recall how many colors of Play-Doh you could mix into a ball before it lost its definable rainbow appeal altogether?

In today's world, you can have truth and I can have truth. Those truths don't have to be the same; they can actually contradict each other and still coexist. What happens when we take this attitude to its logical extreme in our relationship with Jesus?

One fundamental problem with this paradigm is that it doesn't attribute enough intelligence to Jesus and attributes way too much intelligence to me. Being a follower of Christ does not allow me to pick and choose biblical principles that fit my lifestyle and disregard those that don't. Instead, it's imperative I understand that obedience and faith are crucial to following a master. If I follow Christ's commands only when I agree with them or they feel right, I have no longer committed my life to a person but to a religious philosophy with as much substance as that bag of cheese puffs. It may taste good, but soon the cells in my body will be starving for something more. I need the rich, undiluted nourishment of God's Word!

Would Jesus Use a Whip?

Of course, challenging dogma and truth does allow me the freedom to bring different ideas to the table, regardless of where I'm having dinner. For instance, I remember sitting on a five-person BDSM (Bondage Discipline Sado-Masochism) panel during Freedom Week at a major university. (Now *there's* a group I don't normally hang out with.) My sex-education background made me an "expert" for the potentially lively discussions. They knew that "legalistic, dogmatic, and judgmental Christians" would show up to talk about hell and stuff. Not realizing my faith background, they wanted me there to give academic credibility to their atypical sexual practices.

There I was on stage in my Eddie Bauer sweatshirt with a gal to my right wearing tight black lingerie and a dog collar with spikes on it. She held a little black leather whip. To my left was a swank middle-aged man who could have doubled as a GQ cover model but who regularly found sexual relief in BDSM practices.

At first I felt like I had been transported into a bad episode of *The Jerry Springer Show,* but eventually people began to ask serious questions. As the seventy-five people in the room fired questions to the panel, I felt the air change. Then all hell broke loose. Ms. Dominatrix to my right decided to mention that she attended church. As if someone had just fired the first shot at Gettysburg, accusations started flying back and forth about hell, purity, the Bible, and even something about hair color.

I shrank down in my chair and silently prayed something like, *Uh, Jesus, I'm not sure this is a place you would be sitting, but if you found yourself in my place right now, what would you say?*

Before I could get an answer, the voice of the moderator aroused me from my retreat: "Professor Sandras, perhaps you can shed some light on this heated topic."

A response fell out of my mouth: "It seems when it comes to religion and sexuality, all of you came with more ammo to shoot at each other than with sensitivity to hear each other."

The whole room put down their verbal and theological guns and got back to a certain level of civility (as civil as one can be at a BDSM panel). I wish I could tell you that I got to stand up and preach the gospel and the entire room came forward weeping and repenting to an altar call. But in reality, that group was more interested in whips and chains than they were in forgiveness and mercy. However, after the meeting I had a wonderful conversation with my churchgoing dominatrix friend. We talked of the differences between fitting the Bible into our way of life and fitting our way of life into the Bible. We both left feeling stretched in our faith and more aware of the brokenness we tend to bring into our defense of what we believe.

The Truth Is Out There

If done with the right attitude, this new era of exploration allows, even encourages, an open dialogue between faiths and practices. This gives me the freedom to trust Christ as Master not because it's the only option I have been given but because he has shown himself to be the *best option* I have been given.

Cooperating with Jesus is a real choice with real consequences, not something I can slide into by default because I live in a Christian ghetto. Dialogue with unbelievers lets me explore the plethora of ideas out there and find that Jesus really did know what he was talking about. Indeed, Jesus is the Master of Life and is still looking for apprentices in this world. He is looking for people who attribute divine intelligence to him, not just in religious matters but in every matter of their human journey.

I have not been outsmarted by apologetics or outwitted by evangelistic tracts. I have chosen to follow Jesus because my defenses were out-loved by the reality of his presence in my life; I've experienced the evidence that Jesus really does know everything there is about living life, this life, more abundantly.

So we wrestle between two paradigms of truth. I believe, as agent Muldar of *The X-Files* does, that "the truth is out there." I also believe that when the Master Jesus said he is the Truth, he was, well, telling the truth. Thus, the substance of my faith will not be found in definitions, theories, and doctrine but in a person—the person of Christ, who has been known and studied for generations and yet still remains a mystery two thousand years later.

Systematic theology has given us a map, a way to stay on track in this pursuit. Our new cultural spirituality gives us permission to pursue the mystery of faith, the ability to leave some things unanswered and even drive off the map a bit to see God from a new perspective. To find true faith in Christ, we have the responsibility not to rely either on a stone-cold set of doctrines or on our ever-changing smorgasbord of opinions but to instead actually rely on Christ himself.

With Christ as the Master Gardener and his truth revealed in the Scriptures, I can trust that he knows how to fertilize the soil of my life to enhance God's kingdom in and through me. Of course, this sounds much easier than it is. Many in the past have found themselves playing with snakes or demeaning another race in the name of God. I even saw a bumper sticker recently that said, "Lord, please protect me from your followers."

There's a danger of throwing good theology out the window when we slam the door on dogma. The best way I've found to prevent that is to stay true to God's story. I must immerse myself in the whole counsel of Scripture, not just my favorite parts. Earlier we

talked about immersing ourselves in God's story so we can improvise proficiently during our own scenes.

Personally, I like to keep the Word of God fresh as I read it. I
don't stick to just one translation of the Bible. Only reading the
King James Version puts too much KJV in my soil and not enough
NLT (New Living Translation). *The Message,* by Eugene Peterson, has
added a new richness to my readings of the epistles and prophets,
while the New International Version and a respectable commentary
have been the mainstay of my preaching for years. Variety in trans-
lations helps me hear the Author's voice in different tones and
rhythms. And when I commit to giving more weight to scholars
than to scoffers, I find it much easier to hold true to the tenets of
the historic Christian faith.

GROWTH POINTS

1. Consider three distinct differences in worship style or practice (such as baptism protocol, music style, or gender issues)
that set your church apart from others. Discover if those
differences are based on absolutes in Scripture, doctrinal
interpretation, or tradition.

2. What are some areas in which you instinctively trust Jesus,
areas you know are "truth"? What are some areas in which you
instinctively turn elsewhere for answers first? Why?

Defragmenting Your Hard Drive

Another element has crept into the soil of my life, subtly hindering
the cooperative friendship with Jesus that I long for. I noticed it one
day as I conditioned my physical heart while simultaneously
neglecting my spiritual one.

As I pedal on the stationary bicycle at my health club, I watch three televisions. The one on my left has the fast-moving ESPN SportsCenter, the middle one has CNN, and my favorite on the right often shows a classic episode of *The Dukes of Hazzard*. Amazing how I can simultaneously keep track of my heart rate, see the stats of every NFL football player on my fantasy team, catch up on the latest stock options I wish I could afford, and cheer on Bo Duke as he rescues Daisy from the clutches of Boss Hogg.

However, when all is said and done, I can't honestly say I am deeply absorbed in any of the experiences. Frankly, watching just one of the programs would probably bore me. After all, I grew up in the first generation in history that spent more hours per day interacting with the glow of the television than with our parents. Like the overworked soil that caused the dust bowls in American farmlands in the 1920s, our minds can get overworked and lose their fertility. Maybe, like me, you have grown up creating bonsai soil and haven't realized it.

In a plethora of thirty-second snippets, *Sesame Street* taught me the alphabet and how to count to twelve, while *Schoolhouse Rock* taught me all I ever needed to know about conjunctions. Sociologists say that through the wonders of billboards, media ads, and junk mail, I'm asked to process sixteen hundred pieces of information per day. And now that I've grown up, I can simultaneously talk on my cell phone, steer my car to the drive-thru espresso joint, and make a note on my PDA reminding me to spend time with my kids. Okay, so I'm one of *those* drivers.

I get a lot done, or at least I look very busy much of the time. But I have a hard time staying focused on one thing or even one *person* for more than a few minutes. If the soil of my mind is to be rich and fertile, it must have the capacity to hold whatever nutrients Jesus has for it. Unfortunately, my mind is so preoccupied with little and big things that nothing stays in focus for long. Thoughts dance around in my head like a television remote gone rabid.

This became glaringly obvious during my first attempt to experience an ancient practice that is growing in popularity today. I visited a Taizé-style service at a small Episcopal church in my community. The historical Taizé is a tiny village in the hills of Burgundy in eastern France. Since the early 1940s, it has been the home of an ecumenical monastic community of monks whose contemplative prayer is at the center of their lives.

Today, visitors of all ages and backgrounds go to Taizé on a pilgrimage to participate in international meetings of prayer and reflection. The musical style at Taizé services uses short phrases with simple melodic units that anyone can readily memorize. This style of service is increasing popular and is a natural outgrowth of the movement to renew the Christian contemplative tradition. Each service is at times quiet and meditative, and at other times joyous and exuberant. Prayers, psalms, readings, and reflections alternate with choral and other musical works and the distinctive congregational music known simply as Taizé.

Jesus, remember me when you come into your kingdom.
Jesus, remember me when you come into your kingdom.[2]

As I knelt in the candlelit room chanting, "Come, Holy Spirit" (in Latin), I was transported back to fourteenth-century France. I sensed the presence of God, felt the cool stone walls of the cathedrals, smelled the smoky candles, and resonated to the simplicity of a life dedicated to Christ. This was one of those ancient paths I had been searching for! God had never been more tangibly near to me; my soul hadn't felt more alive in years! I wanted to stay wrapped up in this time-warp ecstasy forever.

I'm not sure exactly when it occurred, but as I was kneeling there having this meaningful spiritual experience, I found myself thinking about a really awesome cell phone I had seen at Staples earlier in the day. I began working out in my head how I could justify the expense on my pastor's budget with my finance committee, deciding which color faceplate would look coolest on it, how many minutes in the plan I should sign up for . . .

What a shame. I'm sure my monastic brothers would have been appalled. My thoughts were fragmenting. I just didn't have enough free space in my head, or my heart, to store the experience of such an intimate moment with Christ. The soil in my mind was causing the presence of God to evaporate like a raindrop on a clay-hardened desert landscape. In other words, perhaps my soul was much like the hard drive on my laptop. It was in need of some serious defrag work.

The help function on my computer explains, "A file that is too large for a single location on a disk is fragmented and stored in any free space on the disk. You can use fragmented files, but your computer takes longer to access them. Disk Defragmenter rearranges the files and free space on your disk. Files open more quickly because they are stored in adjacent units, and free space is consolidated."[3]

We have become so used to fragmented thoughts, snippets of information, and sound bites that carry entire ideologies that the idea of disciplining our minds and bodies toward God means something far different from what it meant in ancient days. Developing meaningful faith still takes discipline, focus, and intent. Meditation, study, and silence can work like rototillers on the hardened soil of our souls in order to make them more receptive to the life-giving Word of God.

Even within my Sunday services, where free caffeine and pastries add to the chaotic buzz of a few hundred people, we plan a ten-minute segment of meditation or stillness at some point during our time together. We do it to practice the discipline of silence and to perhaps even hear the whisper of God. It tills the soil of our community and allows the Word of God to soak in.

Ask the Holy Spirit to defragment your thoughts, and then participate in the experience of seeking God. Build upon it daily. Refuse to settle for a *Sesame Street* understanding of an infinite God. Embrace solace as you choose solitude in your week. Pursue study, pursue worship, pursue intimacy with your God, and you will find that you are in turn pursuing a deepening friendship with Jesus. Not doing those things keeps the soil barren and stunts your ability to bear fruit. And as we will discuss next, it prevents the Holy Spirit from "reigning" upon you.

GROWTH POINTS

1. This will seem a bit bizarre, but try it. Find a place of solitude. Turn off all the noise you possibly can. Dim the lights and light a candle. Stare at the candle, and ask the Holy Spirit to teach you something through that candle. Could you stay focused? Could you listen? Is this a discipline you need in your pursuit?

2. Explore two aspects of God's character that interest you. Here are some verses to jump-start your thought processes:

> Joshua 23:16 – God's wrath
> Psalm 136 – God's faithfulness
> Daniel 4:25 – God's sovereignty
> Ephesians 3:17-19 – God's love

Ask Jesus to show you these aspects of his character today. Ask him to turn your head knowledge into real knowledge.

CHAPTER 5

FEEL
THE
REIGN

I REMEMBER HOW CLOSE God's presence seemed to me early in my walk with Him. I could see and feel him in just about everything I experienced.

Back then, I could feel the power of God's Word as it was preached on Sunday morning and penetrated my soul. Now those same messages trigger my critical thinking skills as I evaluate the speaker.

Back then, as I saw the outcast on the street, mercy and compassion flooded over me so strongly that I felt I had no choice but to go and minister to his needs. Now I often see homeless people as distractions from the Bible study or church meeting I must attend.

Back then, I felt God's power flow through me as I prayed for the sick and saw them healed. Now I teach Bible passages about healing, reminiscing about the glory days and subtly communicating that it is enough to only believe it could happen.

Time and "maturity" have trained many of us to live on the minimum of God's presence and still appear healthy. That's disastrous! We should thirst after God and let that longing for his presence cause us to drink from the well that never runs dry. Don't settle for the measly Dixie Cup containers that others have told you are enough to hold God's presence until he returns. Go and find every size and variety of container you can and keep asking God to fill them. He is not stingy with his presence in your life. Ask for it, soak in it, and share it with others. Get under the spout where the power flows out.

We all know that plants need moisture to survive. Even bonsai trees must have water. But the bonsai gardener gives the tree just enough water to keep it alive. Gradually, he trains it to live on very little water and yet be satisfied. Amazingly, a bonsai's foliage can appear green and healthy even though its insides are nearly as parched as a desert wasteland. Likewise, we may look healthy on the outside and yet have arid souls within.

Paul told us, "Do not get drunk on wine, which leads to debauchery. Instead, be filled with the Spirit" (Ephesians 5:18). The prophet Joel wrote,

"I will pour out my Spirit on all people.
Your sons and daughters will prophesy,
    your old men will dream dreams,
    your young men will see visions." (Joel 2:28)

Notice the words "be filled" and "pour" in these passages. If that's not enough, Jesus promises that when we are connected to him, out of our bellies Living Water will gush forth (see John 7:37-39).

These passages don't imply a trickling or eyedropperful of God's Spirit. We aren't supposed to live on the minimum of the refreshing presence of the Holy Spirit and the tangible mentoring of our Master Jesus. Our lives must be deeply and desperately connected to the wellspring of life. We must be experiencing the Father, Son, and Holy Spirit regularly and deeply if we are to thrive.

Experiential and Intellectual

When we talk about going to church to experience the presence of God, we aren't talking about just a nice social group. Our faith communities need to be places where the Holy Spirit is known, recognized, and felt. Not just in a hyped-up, jumpin'-and-jiggin' sort of way in which perspiration is equated with sanctification. We need God's presence to descend on us like rain and produce true inward change and kingdom growth. Why is it, then, that so much of the church seems addicted to Sunday morning entertainment and aesthetic eye candy?

Are we truly experiencing the Holy Spirit in our midst?

The early church seemed to be more dependent on power from on high than on entertainment. Today we often are more concerned with how we, the church, are influencing human affairs on behalf of Christian principles than we are in fulfilling the Great Commission. Our early church brothers and sisters may not have been mighty or noble, but they were endued with power from on high!

Think about the last time (if ever) you recall the Lord's presence filling a meeting you were attending. What happened? How were people responding? What did you want to do? I'm not talking about participating in some Pentecostal poser party, where there is pressure to stop, flop, and roll whether you feel God's leading or not. I've been there and done that. Nor am I talking about a conservative culture of control where the Holy Spirit is expected to toe the line—our line. It goes deeper than style or denomination. It's about openness and desire.

I find it interesting that in most of our churches today, God's presence is associated with joy, feeling good, and enthusiasm. Now I am *not* saying that these things aren't healthy or part of the Christian experience. But we should also emphasize that brokenness and repentance are more common with the initial presence of God than are jubilation and the monetary offerings that follow. Conviction, repentance, and freedom should be tangible experiences in the life of a church body (and my personal body), not just doctrinal conclusions.

Start praying for reign! Admit you're parched and ask the Holy Spirit to bring you more of his tangible presence. As the individual goes, so goes the church. So don't wait for your faith community to change before you start seeking more in your worship experiences. Experiencing God is an attitude, not just an event or theological construct.

You can do this if you let Jesus change you first. Repent often and keep short accounts with God. Allow brokenness and exaltation to share the same bedroom in your life. Let your experiences of God's presence be evident in your actions. It may actually become contagious. God likes both broken things and restored things. Our lives should tangibly encounter the reality of both.

Earth, Wind, or Fire

The town in which I live sits between the waters of the Puget Sound and the majestic Olympic Mountains. The elevation change on a simple drive can go from sea level to four thousand feet in just a few miles. Thus, my little community has its share of steep hills, like the famous San Francisco. Sometimes while driving I imagine myself as Starsky (of *Starsky and Hutch* fame) flying over those sudden crests in the road, chasing some pimp in a low-riding Cadillac. That's usually when my wife says to slow down and stop talking that eighties trash talk because we've got our children in the car.

When my children were younger, we played another fun (and safer) game as we approached the crest of a hill. I would try to convince my little tykes that the road was ending and we were going to fall off the edge of the world. It didn't take much convincing, and often my four-year-old son's eyes would get huge as he tried to stretch to see over the hood to glimpse the apparently disappearing road ahead.

With a quizzical and apprehensive expression, he'd look at Mom as if to ask, "Dad's just kidding, right?" Then before you'd know it, we would crest the hill and start our descent, with an entire road in front of us. My kids have learned (even without therapy) that though the road appears to end, they can count on it being there every time.

Such a simple realization can transform how a kid feels about driving with his father. As adults, we take for granted an understanding of line of sight, but for children it's a new discovery. In a similar way, Christopher Columbus had to challenge the prevailing philosophies of his day in order to sail the oceans blue in 1492. What lay beyond the ocean's horizon was as much a mystery as it was a magnet for this explorer and his crew. Though the idea that they believed the earth was flat is largely a modern myth, the boundaries of exploration were still barriers to these early global nomads.

Journeys like Columbus's changed the way we perceived the world's boundaries. People were suddenly willing to venture farther and discover new lands they never dreamed existed. Now the sun didn't disappear past the horizon; instead, it beckoned those with the desire to follow. New worlds opened up when the horizons were expanded. A dramatic shift in the boundaries we place on ourselves can do that to us.

Europeans had to change their view of the world after Columbus, and their view of the universe exploded when Copernicus proved that the earth and planets revolve around the sun. In the same way, my universe must get a whole lot bigger in order for Jesus to fit into it. The angst comes because I have become so accustomed to *the Son revolving around me* that often I can't make the shift. I long for my life to reflect the words of Michael Frye's song "Be The Centre":

Jesus, be the centre
Be my source, be my light, Jesus,
Be the fire in my heart
Be the wind in these sails
Be the reason that I live Jesus, Jesus
Jesus, be my vision
Be my path, be my guide, Jesus[1]

"Jesus, be the fire in my heart!" That reminds me of the guys on their way to Emmaus in Luke's gospel (see Luke 24:13-35). Downcast and disillusioned, they were discussing the Master Jesus' death. Suddenly, Jesus himself appeared. He told them again the story that God had been writing throughout history about the Messiah. They still didn't recognize him until he allowed the eyes of their hearts to be opened. Then they asked each other, "Were not our hearts burning within us while he talked with us on the road and opened the Scriptures to us?" (Luke 24:32).

A bonsai is trained to live on the minimum of the life-giving presence of water. We can't afford such aridness. Whether we use the analogy of the earth revolving around the sun, or the wind of the Spirit, or the "reign" of God, the point is that we must be immersed in God's presence.

A life oriented around Christ not only drinks from the well that never runs dry but also becomes a wellspring of Living Water for others. Sometimes I think the egocentric life (one that revolves around me) dries that well more than anything else, even more than boredom.

An egocentric life puts me in the quagmire of self-provision, self-procreation, and self-preservation. In other words, the lust of the eyes, the lust of the flesh, and the pride of life drive my life. None of these allows God's presence to reign in my life.

To truly develop a cooperative friendship with Jesus, our fundamental orientation must change. We've got to learn to abide, or live, in Christ. Now that's a feel-good concept that often has very little reality in our everyday lives. Jesus said it this way:

> "*Abide* in me, and I in you. As the branch cannot bear fruit by itself, unless it *abides* in the vine, neither can you, unless you *abide* in me. I am the vine, you are the branches. He who *abides* in me, and I in him, he it is that bears much fruit, for apart from me you can do nothing. If a man does not *abide* in me, he is cast forth as a branch and withers; and the branches are gathered, thrown into the fire and burned. If you *abide* in me, and my words *abide* in you, ask whatever you will, and it shall be done for you." (John 15:4-7, RSV, emphasis added)

Seven times in only four verses, Jesus encourages us to abide. Actually, it's more of an expectation. He expects everyone who professes him as Master to make him our home. Should we decide not to abide, Jesus presents us with a picture of a whole lot of bonsai trees getting tossed into the fire. We've got to find a way to abide. It is the only way to solve the problem in our souls. It is the only way to stay tapped into the life-giving water of God's presence.

The Word of God is essential to proper abiding. Did you notice how on the road to Emmaus, the disciples' hearts were burning because Jesus opened the Scriptures to them? And how in John, Jesus exhorts us to have his words abide in us? The fertile soil of our minds is kept moist by the presence of the Author himself.

People whose lives are oriented around Christ don't just study the Bible to be smarter. They see that every single page of the New Testament is stained with the crimson blood of Jesus himself. Suddenly, the Bible isn't just a text to be studied but a source of life for a withering branch. Unless the Holy Spirit brings the Word to life, study will only make you smarter, not healthier.

Abiding in Christ isn't just knowing more about Jesus but knowing Jesus more. It involves cultivating a moment-to-moment awareness of his involvement in our lives. In chapter 9 we'll see that this cultivation is actually an act of worship.

GROWTH POINTS

1. Outside of a religious context, think of someone you regularly abide (live) with or someplace where you regularly abide. What makes abiding with that person or at that place attractive to you? What do you get out of it? What does it cost you? What similarities does the Holy Spirit show you through John 15:4-7?

2. Take some time and ask Jesus if there are some horizons in your life that he wants you to go beyond and if there are some anchors that are keeping you from the journey.

Experiencing God in Today's Kitchens

I worked as a waiter throughout my ten years of higher education. One restaurant stands out in particular. It wasn't the food, or even the patrons, that made it unique in my life. It was the life lesson Jesus taught me there.

My wife and I were living in Seattle at the time. I had just finished my master's degree in Human Development and Family Studies, and we were helping some friends start a church. We ventured into the birthplace of both grunge music and almighty Microsoft only weeks before having our first child. With résumé in hand, I went job hunting, certain that I could work at a local community college or with any number of human resource firms.

Door after door slammed shut, sometimes with my foot still in the gap trying to reason with them. Granted, Seattle's economy was in quite a slump that year, but I believed I was something special. I was down to one last great opportunity—a consulting firm that gave antidiscrimination courses all over the country, including one for the Goodwill Games on the topic of race (as in nationality/ creed) relations. Out of six hundred applicants, I had made it to the top twenty. Still, desperate times called for desperate measures, so I took a job waiting tables at a local barbecued-ribs joint. *Surely,* I thought, *it will be just a couple of days and I'll land the consulting job.*

Days turned into weeks, and weeks into two months, as the interview process dragged on. I went to their corporate office on the twenty-eighth floor of a beautiful downtown skyscraper that overlooked scenic Elliot Bay. We talked about six-figure consulting contracts, and I responded to countless scenarios assessing my ability to train people in diversity and teamwork.

Each time the interview ended, I would hop in the elevator, look at my watch, and realize I had only twenty minutes to get to the restaurant before my shift started. Like Superman changing back to Clark Kent, I found myself changing uniforms for another chaotic six-hour dinner shift.

Emotionally, I began to crumble. The job itself wasn't bad and the people were nice, but I felt this job was stealing my time from the church I was helping launch. More important, it was robbing me of precious time with my newborn daughter. I felt I was better than this job but was stuck in this grind nonetheless.

There are pinnacle moments in the story that God writes into our lives that sometimes take pages to lead up to. This night was one of them, and it all began with an empty coffee cup. My complaining customer made sure I and everyone else at the table knew how tragic his life had become because I had forgotten to refill his cup.

I could feel the volcano inside me about to erupt. *Get a life, you dork. You're worried about a cup of coffee and I'm barely paying rent, haven't spent but twenty minutes with my daughter today, and wonder if God still cares about my calling.*

Of course, comments like that aren't good for one's tips, so I bottled it up, smiled, and poured his coffee with a hint of disdain. As I walked back toward the kitchen, I muttered under my breath, "God, this job sucks. I want something better than this."

I'm still not sure what happened, but it seemed as if time stood still. The clanging of dishes and constant motion of cooks and servers ceased. As I stood there in silence, I heard God's voice: "It is not the job, my son. It is your attitude. Let it be like that of Christ Jesus."

Okay, so perhaps I spent too much time in the walk-in freezer that day, but it was if I was transported to another place. There I saw the Master Jesus washing feet. The voice of wisdom said, "You know, Eric, washing feet was one of the most mundane and disgusting jobs a man could perform in those days. Nobody volunteered to do it, and nobody praised those who did. That is, of course, until Jesus did it. From that point on, history has never seen footwashing the same way."

Crash! The sound of a dish shattering on the floor shook me to consciousness. I had dropped the plate I was carrying, but it didn't matter. The Holy Spirit had just showed me the very path Jesus had walked when he washed feet, and now I saw the path I could choose while I waited tables. Suddenly, I really believed that the very presence of the kingdom of God could be a part of my table-waiting experience. It was no longer about *where* I was; it was about *who* I was!

From, To, and Through

Wouldn't it be amazing to alter the very way we see and interact with this world so we responsed to life more Christlike than "me-like"? What if it became more natural to live a life "holy and pleasing to God" rather than to live a life wholly pleasing to us? Wouldn't I have a much greater chance of becoming an apprentice to Jesus than just a bonsai believer?

> For from him and through him and to him are all
> things.
> To him be the glory forever! Amen.
>
> Therefore, I urge you, brothers, in view of God's
> mercy, to offer your bodies as living sacrifices, holy
> and pleasing to God—this is your spiritual act of wor-
> ship." (Romans 11:36–12:1)

This passage by brother Paul may seem awkward when read this way because most of us have been raised with a big "12" that interrupts these verses. But the chapter number wasn't there when Paul wrote his letter. We have been trained to see the world through "I" perspective, even as we are trying to live out one of the most powerful Scriptures in the New Testament. Let me explain.

God's blessings are meant to be circular. How often have we prayed for God's blessings to grace our families or churches? We pray for more of God's financial provision, more of his healing power, more of his mercy. We pray for him to enlarge our territory and expand our borders. Now there is nothing wrong with that type of prayer. God wants to bless us. He loves his kids and desires to see they are cared for. God, however, may be content for you to drive an '83 Dodge even though you think you need an Eddie Bauer–edition Pathfinder. Regardless of the level of blessings we have been given, we are all called to offer ourselves as living sacrifices to God.

But what does that really mean?

We have been dining at the table of consumerism for so long that we have begun to think it means we need to sacrifice so that God is obligated to give us more. Haven't we all met self-absorbed Christians who seem to be more concerned about what God owes them than what God has already given them? They seem to have a business arrangement of sorts. Consumerism says it's all about me: my comfort, my needs, my blessings. Paul said it's all about God.

From him: Yes, God is the source of all of my blessings and gifts.

Through him: The sacrifices I make, the ministries I start, and the support I receive need to be done through his power and vision. But I must not stop there. If I stop there, the end product is about me.

To him: Instead, we are to complete the circle and ensure that all glory and honor go to him—forever! Amen.

Not long after my dish-shattering experience with the Holy Spirit in the restaurant, I learned that I had made it to number two on the list for the consulting job before they gave it to someone else. It didn't matter much by then. Four months after that, we moved to the next city on our academic journey: Corvallis, Oregon.

But before we left Seattle, the staff at the restaurant threw a party for me. The manager said there was something about the way I cared that made the whole restaurant a better place. One of the waitresses made a statement as I was leaving that has stuck with me for ten years: "Eric, I know this sounds strange, but I don't think I'll ever see this job the same way again. Thanks." Wisdom's words had been true. And as for that waitress, she still sends my family Christmas cards.

Making the Mundane Sacred

Brother Lawrence (1611–1691) understood the principle of living from, to, and through Christ better than most. He was already fifty-five years old when he became a lay member of the Discalced Carmelite order in the sprawling city of Paris. For the final twenty-five years of his human journey, he worked in seeming obscurity in the kitchen of his order. Yet Brother Lawrence had this uncanny ability to turn even the most mundane and disrespected job into a life-giving experience with his Lord. Because he saw everything as coming from God, through God, and to God, nothing seemed trivial. In fact, he tried to live in the habitual presence of God. This orientation made him one of the most fake-free followers of Christ the church has ever known.[2]

God's tangible presence was not something Brother Lawrence hoped to receive someday after his life was over. He recognized that the presence of God, the abundant life Jesus talked of, was for the here and now. Unlike bonsai believers who learn to live on the minimum of God's presence, he was never content with the desert but wanted constantly to live in the reign of the Holy Spirit. This ordinary man showed what it means to abide with Christ in our everyday lives.

Imagine for a moment how your daily grind at the office or in the home would change if you truly got hold of this perspective.

You may want to read Brother Lawrence's collection of letters, called *The Practice of the Presence of God.* Here is an excerpt to whet your appetite:

> Yet I think it proper to inform you after what manner I consider myself before God, whom I behold as my King.
>
> I consider myself as the most wretched of men, full of sores and corruption, and who has committed all sorts of crimes against his King. Touched with a sensible regret, I confess to Him all my wickedness, I ask His forgiveness, I abandon myself in His hands that He may do what He pleases with me. The King, full of mercy and goodness, very far from chastising me, embraces me with love, makes me eat at His table, serves me with His own hands, gives me the key of His treasures; He converses and delights Himself with me incessantly, in a thousand and a thousand ways, and treats me in all respects as His favorite.[3]

Don't we need to learn how to see ourselves in God's presence that way? Brother Lawrence gives us some key ingredients to experiencing the tangible presence of God: confession, forgiveness, conversation, and proper perspective. Could this man of the kitchen find God's presence in such a role if he were around today? Could the kingdom of God still bear this kind of fruit in the trees planted in God's orchard today?

Drenched in Reign

What in your life is grinding your emotions to a pulp? What are you stuck in that seems to show no mercy to the things you wish you could be doing? Is resentment building in your soul?

Perhaps Jesus is giving you the chance to experience his kingdom. Are you so consumed with trying to do something *for* God that you aren't allowing room just to *be* God's? You can take the most mundane and even despised task and turn it into a glorifying kingdom experience. This perspective opens the heavens so that God's life-giving reign can satiate your emotional dryness. It's a perspective of humility and surrender. If you find yourself at such a place, treasure this time. Heed Paul's words:

> Your attitude should be the same as that of Christ Jesus:
>
> Who, being in very nature God,
>   did not consider equality with God something to be
>   grasped,
> but made himself nothing. (Philippians 2:5-7)

GROWTH POINTS

1. What is one of the most mundane tasks you do every week? Is it doing the laundry, making photocopies, scrubbing floors? Ask Jesus to give you the attitude of Brother Lawrence about this task.

2. Ponder the times when you have sensed the tangible presence of God. Where were you? What was going on in your heart? Are there any aspects of such encounters that you could carry over to the times when you feel nowhere near God's presence?

CHAPTER 6

UNLEASH
YOUR
DNA

HAVE YOU EVER NOTICED the contorted shapes of trees growing around timberline in the mountains or on the coast? Wind and weather have twisted them in the most unusual ways. They have adapted to the harshest of conditions in order to survive. In fact, what they have endured often makes them that much more beautiful.

That same weathered look draws many bonsai artists. The gardener uses wire to wrap the trunk and branches to force the tree to grow in directions he chooses, not in the ways it is naturally designed to grow. The bonsai artist blends the wires inconspicuously around the trunk so the unnatural growth doesn't appear contrived and manipulated. The artist is in control, and the tree must conform to the pattern he determines. However, the rest of the world needs to be convinced that such growth was natural and necessary.

The wires that bend a bonsai believer operate both on a cultural level and on a local church level. Once again, the goal is to have the appearance of a healthy relationship with Christ without the reality. But if we want to be the real thing, we need to snap those wires and let ourselves and everyone around us grow into the unique persons our spiritual DNA designed us to be.

The Wires of Western Culture

My friends Dr. Suuqiina (Sue-key-na) and Qaumaniq (Kwaw-ma-neek) encountered such wires at the cultural level. Dr. Suuqiina is a native Inuit from Alaska. When he was growing up, our government took hundreds of Inuit children and "adopted" them into Anglo homes in order to train them to be culturally acceptable and fit a preconceived idea of what an "American" ought to be. Suuqiina was one of those children torn from his brother and family and raised in an Anglo-Christian home. There he was taught that God made a mistake when he made natives and that his former language and traditions where at best irrelevant and at worst demonic. The goal was to get him to speak the *right* language, use the *right* manners, and honor the *right* traditions. Over the years, he was forced to grow in unnatural ways and learn to be someone he inherently knew he wasn't—a proper white Anglo-Christian boy.

Thankfully, Jesus has the power to redeem all things, including culture, and today Dr. Suuqiina (his doctorate is in theology) and his Cherokee wife, Qaumaniq, travel the world helping people learn to worship the Creator Jesus in ways that are culturally natural to them and uncompromisingly biblical. They work tirelessly, untangling the web of cultural restrictions that have been placed on First Nations peoples. Those restrictions make people look like the worshipers the establishment wants, not like what God created.

Since my introduction to Dr. Suuqiina and Qaumaniq, I have been able to build relationships with and learn from other cultural oracles to the Christian world. Recently, messianic Jews Arni and Yonit Klein of Emmaus Way ministries in Tel Aviv further expanded my horizons. My spine tingled and my spirit leapt as Arni blew his *sopar* and prayed over my city and church. He told how he learned to honor his heritage and not bend to the "Western euro" traditions of Christianity that said there was only one way to pray or worship.

I even have had the opportunity to worship God within the powerful warrior dance tradition of New Zealand's Maori people. Many Maoris have come to love Jesus and worship him in ways natural to their culture, in spite of attempts by Western missionaries to acculturate them.

Whether on a cultural scale or home-church scale, we must open our eyes to see what God has naturally put in a person or people. We can then bless and release it to become what it was intended to become. Paul wrote, "It was he who gave some to be apostles, some to be prophets, some to be evangelists, and some to be pastors and teachers, to prepare God's people for works of service, so that the body of Christ may be built up until we all reach unity in the faith and in the knowledge of the Son of God and become mature, attaining to the whole measure of the fullness of Christ" (Ephesians 4:11-13).

The goal should be not to make everyone look and act like each other but to help us all become more like Christ. We can be Christlike whether we are dressed in a suit and tie, buckskin and feathers, or black leather and spikes. It has little to do with our style and almost everything to do with our heart and the freedom we give the creative hand of God to work in our lives.

We can break free of the wires that bind us and attain the "whole measure of the fullness of Christ." But we must realize the wires are there and how they seek to shape us.

Bowing at the Altar of Consumerism

Isn't it amazing to watch how quickly the world has been changing over the past three decades? We watched the Soviet Union and
the Berlin Wall collapse. We are seeing China move toward a free-
market economy. Nations all over the world are finding freedom in
democracy or at least less-restrictive markets. Even the golden
arches of McDonald's are popping up in cities where we would
have thought unthinkable a decade ago.

But is our culture of consumerism the end-all of cultural bliss?
Might we find ourselves seeing the promises of consumerism
chipped and broken down like the Berlin Wall? Are we bowing to
a god as lifeless as communism?

The pressure of consumerism is like the hidden wires that force
the bonsai to bend in a way it was not originally intended. To the
untrained eye such wires go unnoticed, but once you spot them
you get the feeling that something is not quite right. Consumerism
forces us to bow—not to Jesus in worship and honor but to the
golden statue of our culture.

I noticed the hidden wires in my psyche one day as my wife
and I were paying homage to the great wall of toilet seats at Home
Depot. We were replacing our 1940s commode that refilled itself
every twenty minutes. I had no idea that this great country of ours
produced so many choices in toilet bowls, toilet tanks, and toilet
seats.

After taking an hour to choose the bowl and tank, we stared at
a massive wall display of thirty or forty toilet seats. They had the
avocado green, soft foam, padded ones like my grandmother used
to have; the fancy solid oak ones like wealthy people get to sit on;
and the countless colors and styles of plastic we regular folk put
our haunches on. We ruled out the seashell style but couldn't make

up our minds between the antique oval and the off-white standard. Suddenly I became aware of how precious my behind was and what others might think if our toilet seat wasn't a good fit with the rest of our decor or their derrieres. We struggled to find the perfect balance between bathroom etiquette and financial savvy. We were beginning to bow at the altar of consumerism.

Most industries don't even refer to us as people anymore. We are *consumers,* and we have been taught that we were created to consume. We are told never to be satisfied, at least not for long. Our felt needs take precedence over our virtues. This relentless message that we are consumers before we are persons encourages a me-first attitude that stunts the growth of God's kingdom within us. We begin to see others as commodities and soon are unable to bless what God is doing in them because it interferes with what we might be able to get from them.

Though the Bible tells me to bear fruit such as self-control and sacrifice, my feet are firmly planted in the soil of instant gratification. In this world, I sometimes wonder if I'm actually not more of a life-taking "consumer" than I am a life-giving Christian.

It's much more natural for me to see people for what they have, what they are wearing, and what they do than it is to see people for what eternity holds for them or what God is doing in their lives. I tend to interpret circumstances by asking, *How is this going to affect me?* not *What does this mean for Jesus' purpose in them?*

So how do we change from being consumer oriented to being truth oriented, fulfilling our true created destiny in Christ?

The Matrix Meets Bernard

I found my answer in the film *The Matrix.* There our hero, Neo, learns that the world he thought was real is only a complex system of computer simulations controlled by artificial intelligence. But Neo was created for something different and over time discovers that he can live within the confines of this system without bowing to all its rules. Toward the end of the movie, after a resurrection experience of sorts, he finds that he has the power not only to bend the rules but also to change them. This discovery enables him to begin to free others who are trapped within the matrix.

I too have been born into a system so all-encompassing that, unless I'm taught to see differently, I won't even know a different reality exists. I can learn to live within this world but function by a different set of rules. I even have a mandate to set others free after I have become free myself.

A thousand years before *The Matrix,* a real person made a similar discovery. His name was Bernard of Clairvaux. Born in AD 1090, Bernard was the third son of a Burgundian nobleman. His brothers were trained as soldiers, but Bernard from his youth believed he was called to pursue the mystery of Christ.

One Christmas Eve, when he was just a child, he dreamed about the infant Christ lying in the manger. That experience set him on a journey to discover the essence of this core truth: "The Word became flesh and made his dwelling among us. We have seen his glory, the glory of the One and Only, who came from the Father, full of grace and truth" (John 1:14).

After a period of prayer for guidance, Bernard decided, at age twenty-two, to enter the monastery of Citeaux, a founding house of the Trappist order. The Trappist monks practiced a stricter lifestyle than the Benedictines, from whom their order was born. Bernard persuaded some of his brothers, one uncle, and twenty-six other men to join him. They were the first novices that Citeaux had had for several years.

It didn't take long for Citeaux's abbot to recognize Bernard's leadership and passion. After only three years, the abbot sent the young Bernard, as the head of a band of twelve monks, to found a new monastic community at Vallée d'Absinthe, or Valley of Bitterness, in the Diocese of Langres. Bernard named it Claire Vallée, of Clairvaux, and history tells us that from that point on, the names of Bernard and Clairvaux joined as one.[1]

His first year was rough. His monastic brothers had no time to gather provisions for the winter and lived almost exclusively on roots and barley bread. Through it all, Bernard imposed such severe discipline that his followers became discouraged and began to question their commitment to the movement. Seeking the Master Jesus through prayer and petition, Bernard realized his errors and became more lenient.

Bernard also developed a reputation of challenging other church leaders in their views of the Scriptures. He felt that many had abandoned the great mysteries of faith and the passionate pursuit of love and holiness in order to pursue a more rationalistic approach to the Bible and God. He was swimming against a religious tide that was drawing people of faith toward hypocrisy.

Bernard's perspective moves me to ask, *Could a significant part of faith be found in mystery instead of understanding? Is it possible to stare in wonder or bow in awe, regardless of understanding?*

Perhaps we can hold fast to faith while admitting that even the church doesn't have all the answers. We have worked so hard to understand faith that for many of us it has transformed itself into rational argument. Yet I have found that the mystery and my lack of understanding of God's ways make my growth more of an adventure and less of a calculated manufacturing process.

Growing Toward Love

Clairvaux's reputation spread across Europe. Many new monks joined the community, and many persons visited or wrote letters for spiritual advice. As Bernard continued to pursue the mysteries of faith, his influence grew. Though not without controversy, his order, called Cistercian, founded sixty monasteries during his lifetime.

During this struggle and pursuit, Bernard wrote a treatise called "On the Love of God," in which he expounded four levels, or degrees, of love. I believe Bernard's model can loosen the wires of consumerism that bend and bind us, and can enable us to grow toward the Son again.

Love Level 1

The first level of love is what Bernard describes as *love of the self, for self's sake*. This is where most of us live. This is the wire that wraps tightly around our psyche and lifestyles. It stunts our kingdom potential and turns us into beautiful bonsai believers. We appear to love God *when in reality it's all about me*.

When Jesus said, "Love your neighbor as yourself" (Matthew 22:39), he understood the most primitive love within us: *I love me*. Humanistic psychologist Abraham Maslow called this the basic need for survival.[2] Sigmund Freud called it the "ID" that operates by the "pleasure principle."[3] Anyone who has a two-year-old knows it as the Toddler Laws:[4]

1. If I like it, it's mine.
2. If it's in my hand, it's mine.
3. If I can take it from you, it's mine.
4. If I had it a little while ago, it's mine.
5. If it's mine, it must not ever appear to be yours in any way.

6. If I'm doing or building something, all of the pieces are mine.
7. If it looks just like mine, it's mine.
8. If I saw it first, it's mine.
9. If you're playing with something and you put it down, it automatically becomes mine.
10. If it's broken, it's yours.

However you define this love of self for self's sake, it's the fuel that drives our consumer culture. We are bombarded with images that appeal to our primal desires for food, sex, and shelter. But even without those media images, Bernard of Clairvaux saw that human greed, lust, and want spring from our love of self for self's sake.

I don't know how many times I've talked to teens who say, "That's not true. I hate myself! I'm so fat. I'm so ugly. I'm so bad in school." However, statements like those only reinforce Bernard's belief.

"If you truly hated yourself," I often reply, "you'd be glad you're ugly!"

The fact is, we love ourselves and always want this self to be happy and cared for. If it weren't for God's relentless love, we would forever stay absorbed in our self-love. But by grace, some manage to break free of toddlerhood and find the next stage of love.

Love Level 2

The second level of love is the *love of God for self's sake*. Think about it. We often find ourselves in dire situations—nothing seems to be going right. Even with all of our efforts to care for ourselves, we just can't seem to make it. Out of desperation, we call out to God for help. And often, God pulls through for us.

The Greeks had a word for this type of rescue: *soteria*. We usually translate it as *salvation*. Jesus used the word this way when he said, "For whoever wants to *save* his life will lose it, but whoever loses his life for me will find it" (Matthew 16:25, emphasis added). We sing about it this way:

> Amazing grace, how sweet the sound,
> that saved a wretch like me.
> I once was lost, but now am found,
> was blind but now I see.

Welcome to the love of God for self's sake. When we break free of the wires of level one, we should eventually accept God's help to break free of the wires of level two. Still, we've got to pass through this stage on our way to becoming the person we were created to be. Level two says we've come to a point in life when we see that God is real and he does care. He's rescued us from the minor fender benders of life and the major collision we were about to have with hell. We sing countless praise songs that reflect this level of love. We gather around the campfires and reflect on God's goodness in our lives. We share "testimonies." I can just hear the preacher now:

> "Can I get a testimony in the house tonight?"
> "Amen, brother! God came through, and I got a healing from my stomach condition!" shouts Sister Mildred.
> "Amen, Rev! I tithed when I thought I couldn't, and I just received this refund from the IRS!" praises Brother Mel.

Now don't get me wrong. I love testimonies that reflect God's goodness. We need them and should share them with others. My church's mission statement affirms, "We are real people who know and worship a real Jesus, who helps us overcome real problems so we can become real testimonies of his love and faithfulness." Testimonies strengthen our faith, help us get our eyes off of ourselves, and draw others to Christ. They are like billboards on the highway pointing to a greater destination.

Spend a few minutes listening to Christian radio for the message "Love of God for self's sake." Much of our contemporary church culture lives and breathes this air. It's a natural part of the growth process, but if we stop here we will miss so much more of the rich and fruitful growth God wants to provide.

Love Level 3

Abundant fruit grows from level three: *love of God for God's sake.* Bonsai believers are never able to see God as anything but a cosmic bellhop. They ring and expect him to answer. If he comes through, they may even be inclined to leave a 10-percent tip. Such faith is constrained by the wires of consumerism.

But for some, the truths of God's character begin to shape how they perceive both God and life. Some are able, by recognizing God's continual grace, to love him not just for what he has done for them but for who he is. David captured this love when he wrote,

> For the LORD is good and his love endures forever;
>   his faithfulness continues through all generations.
>   (Psalm 100:5)

It is at this level of love that God invites us to pursue the unattainable, fathom the unfathomable, and measure the immeasurable. Paul penned this invitation when he wrote,

And I pray that you, being rooted and established in love, may have power, together with all the saints, to grasp how wide and long and high and deep is the love of Christ, and to know this love that surpasses knowledge—that you may be filled to the measure of all the fullness of God. (Ephesians 3:17-19)

Paul prayed that we could know the love that surpasses knowledge: fathom the unfathomable. Pursuing this knowledge, rather than attaining it in this life, is what matters. Find a place of solitude for a few minutes and ponder the love that is beyond comprehension. Perhaps you'll find that it has less to do with you and what you receive and more to do with Jesus and what he receives from you. If you're ready to launch into the depths of God's love, these notes I wrote in the margins of my Bible may help:

HOW WIDE IS GOD'S LOVE?

► The Pharisees thought it was restricted to people just like them. Jesus said they were wrong.

► God's love is not that narrow; it is wide, so wide that you have never met a person God does not love. (*Have* you?)

HOW LONG IS GOD'S LOVE?

► God's love is so long that it stretches from eternity to eternity.

► God's love is so long that it outlasts any problem I may have.

How high is God's love?

▶ Isaiah 55:9 — God's love is purer, more consistent, more faithful, more just, more than any love any man (except Jesus) has ever known or given.

▶ As I reach up and grasp how high the love of God is, I gain new perspectives on life's problems and blessings.

How deep is God's love?

▶ Corrie ten Boom: "There is no pit so deep that God's love is not deeper still."[5]

▶ So deep that he was born in a manger, lived as a man, and hung naked on a cross, born into the deepest shame of humanity (see Philippians 2:8).

Incredible, isn't it? When we pursue God's love, it just keeps getting wider and longer and deeper and higher. And as love becomes experiential, when its reality becomes evident in my life, *Ping!* I can hear the wires snapping now.

As I walk into a classroom and hear a professor spewing new-age ideologies to students or see a meth dealer selling to some junior-high school kid on the street, do I feel the love of God that is wide enough to encompass even them? Have I ever been so trampled by others or my own choices that it seemed there was no way God's love could reach down and pick me up? When I sin and the response I expect from the church is "How could you?" but the response I hear from God through them is "I still love you," God's love becomes tangible. He deserves love for who he is and not just what he has done for me.

Love Level 4

To live in the third degree of God's love requires more than just an intellectual assent to that belief but a life oriented toward it. And the more I live out my daily existence loving God, the more likely I am to move into Bernard's fourth degree of God's love: *love of self for God's sake.*[6]

Take a moment and reflect on that idea: *the love of self for God's sake.* What do you think Bernard meant?

Most of us would want to switch levels three and four. We believe that ultimately we should love God for God's sake. To love myself for God's sake seems selfish and almost new-ageish. But for a moment, step aside from our cultural assumption that self-love equals self-gratification and self-esteem. I believe Bernard was saying something much more profound—something our cotton-candy–fluffed, self-loving mentality can't grasp without the Holy Spirit's aid—for to live at level four is to be set free from bonsai constraints and to thrive in God's kingdom. Of course, I only give you my interpretation, because I can't honestly say I've made it to that stage yet on my journey toward a truer relationship with Christ.

Go back with me to *The Matrix.* Recall how Neo discovers he can live within the confines of his world's system without bowing to all of its rules. As Neo grows to understand he is different, he learns he can even change the rules. At one point in the movie, Neo no longer sees his surroundings with the eyes he was taught to see with but with "enlightened eyes." He sees the world as it really is—made up of computer binary codes.

This revelation changes how he sees not only his own life but also everyone else's. This Y2K movie and Bernard's Y1K vision meet at the fourth degree of love.

When the reality of our relationship, position, and purpose with Christ get hold of us, our whole lives change. I'm not talking about getting fire insurance just to get to heaven or even suddenly living a moral life here on earth. I should begin to find myself in a state of being that changes me and everyone else around me. Bernard says that few ever reach this place, and even fewer remain there. Still, it's a destination I long for.

Jesus Unwired

Jesus lived at level four, completely free of our world's wires. At one point, he and his disciples were crossing the Sea of Galilee by boat and a storm blew in (see Luke 8:22-25). The Master of all creation slept while the boat was on the verge of being swamped and sinking. The disciples woke him and yelled over the chaos, "Master, Master, we're going to drown!"

This is a prayer—maybe not in our pious religious traditions, but it is a prayer nonetheless. After all, what do you call talking to God? Prayer. That's right. So they prayed for help and got it! They were in trouble and went to God, and he calmed the storm. Isn't that what we're supposed to do? A storm comes, we pray to God for help, and he answers?

Interestingly, when the sea settled, Jesus rebuked his disciples: "Where is your faith?" I've grown up seeing this rebuke in light of the destination. Didn't Jesus say they were going to the other side of the lake? If he said they would make it, then they would make it. But when the storm hit, they thought they were going to drown and became afraid. They forgot that God is bigger than the biggest storms. Yep, there's some great sermon stuff there.

So where is our faith? Shouldn't it be in God's promise to get us to the destination he has determined? They woke Jesus and asked him to do something about the storm—that sounds like faith to me. But Jesus asked, "Where is your faith?" Hadn't the disciples put it in Jesus? Hadn't they given up on their own efforts and "prayed" to God?

Had this happened to any of us today, most would consider it a success story! We made the choice to pray in a desperate situation, and God delivered us. What a testimony we now have! We go around and share with others how we put our faith in God's provision and he came through! Would Jesus have the nerve to ask us, "Where is your faith?"

Let's look at this passage in light of Bernard's fourth degree of love, *the love of self for God's sake*. What if Jesus were trying to teach his apprentices (who were learning to do what Jesus did) that *they* should have commanded the storm to be still? What if Jesus was trying to teach them to see the world from the new perspective of God's kingdom?

As followers of Jesus, *they* could have bent the rules of nature as well! When we are walking in harmony with God's kingdom, there is power to overcome any barrier. This is what a healthy, thriving tree on the banks of God's river looks like. This is so far beyond bonsai that we can scarcely imagine it.

When I truly see myself as God sees me, know my purposes as God intends, and walk in the power that God provides, amazing things happen. I find myself so secure in God's presence that I can be in this world but not of it. I start to act from an eternally new perspective, such as Paul described in his letter to the Ephesians:

> As for you, you were dead in your transgressions and
> sins, in which you used to live when you followed the
> ways of this world and of the ruler of the kingdom of
> the air. . . . But because of his great love for us, God,
> who is rich in mercy, made us alive with Christ even
> when we were dead in transgressions—it is by grace

you have been saved. And God raised us up with
Christ and seated us with him in the heavenly realms
in Christ Jesus." (Ephesians 2:1-2,4-6)

Jesus Christ invites us to begin to see the world from his kingdom perspective—his perspective, his power, his grace. The daily
grind often causes us to lose this perspective. But once you and I
taste the pursuit of love's fourth level, once we experience the
empowering presence of Jesus that fills every fiber of our being and
changes how we interface with this world, we will no longer be
willing to bow to its idols. We will grow in love—not in a selfish
sense, where it's all about me, but in a biblical sense, where it is all
about him. As we undo the wires that constrain us, we will grow
and see new life. Usually, that's when the pruning comes.

GROWTH POINTS

1. Draw a picture of the four levels of God's love. Pay attention
to what form you use: for example, concentric circles, steps, a
line with markers. Why did you choose such a model? Try to
draw it a different way.

2. Take a moment and ask the Holy Spirit to show you where
he sees you in your model. Would you put yourself in the
same place he did? Finally, what growth can you realistically see
over the next six months?

CHAPTER 7

CALL
FORTH
LIFE

FROM VINEYARD OWNERS TO tomato gardeners, most people prune a plant in order to enhance its ability to bear fruit. However, in the bonsai tradition, pruning is done to *limit* fruit production. Whenever the bonsai artist sees life or limbs he doesn't want, he prunes them. He must prune at the first sign of life or else the scarring will be more noticeable. This type of pruning keeps the bonsai small and under complete control.

As I've matured in my faith, it has become easier for me to be a master pruner in other people's lives. Young, idealistic visionaries come to me with entrepreneurial ideas and snip, snip . . . it is so easy for me to find five or six reasons why their ideas won't work. How ironic, because during my days of reckless abandonment for Christ, few things I did *ever* made sense. Yet because God was in them, they always seemed to bear fruit.

Why is it so easy to criticize and so difficult to encourage? I don't know, but if we want to be strong, deeply rooted believers—and help others be the same—we need to put down our pruning shears and learn instead to call forth more life.

Bonsai believers not only exhibit stunted growth themselves but they work hard to keep others there as well. Few things are more frustrating than seeing someone with big fruit on their tree while the fruit on my own tree is small and withered. But in the kingdom of God, when I bless others and sow into their lives, my own harvest increases. Fertile faith doesn't mean just *looking like* a fruitful vineyard; it means *being* a fruitful vineyard.

Is it easier for you to defend the status quo, or the entrepreneurs in your midst? Jesus wants us to be life-nurturing people even when we must point out concerns to others. He said it this way:

"Do not judge, or you too will be judged. For in the same way you judge others, you will be judged." (Matthew 7:1-2)

"If your brother sins against you, go and show him his fault, just between the two of you. If he listens to you, you have won your brother over." (Matthew 18:15)

Breaking the Culture of Conformity

Though we are all called to conform to Christ's image, we are also individuals, each with unique life circumstances and quirks. How a community embraces those differences often determines whether people feel free to be real, or just play the church game—whether they choose to be flourishing trees, or bonsai. Bonsai believers tend to worry not only about how they look but also about how those around them look. The result is communities of people who all look alike.

To truly foster growth in ourselves and others, we need to quit pruning each other to ensure everyone stays under control. We can trust the Holy Spirit to build the forest with a wide variety of trees.

Regarding your house of worship, ask yourself, *Does my community provide an atmosphere of freedom that allows each person to be honest, gives them permission to stumble, and even lets them ask hard questions without the fear of punishment, shame, or rejection? Is it just as okay to say, "I doubt," as it is to say, "I believe," in my house of worship?*

I've seen a powerful phenomenon in many churches. I call it "the culture of conformity." Over time, the members of a church just start looking and acting more alike—not necessarily more like Jesus, but more like whatever the unwritten code of the community is. Whenever someone sprouts an unusual leaf, out come the scissors and snip, snip. . . . People begin to use the same lingo, say prayers with similar vocal inflections, and even project unwritten vibes about which sins are tolerable and which are not.

The coffee was hot and the transparency was thin one morning when this topic came up with one of my mentors, who happens to be a Lutheran pastor. I was sharing with him how subtly conformity can creep into cutting-edge worship movements like Vineyard. For a season, leaders in my movement were actually debating how long worship sets should last on Sunday mornings.

The seeker-sensitive side of our movement thought twenty-five minutes was the max, while others were asserting that "Vineyard" worship was open-ended and spirit-led. Unwittingly, we were bringing conformity to something that was as natural as walking. We were pruning in places where sweeter and more diverse fruit was trying to grow. Finally, our national director admonished us that "Vineyard" worship was simply John Wimber (Vineyard's founder) sitting at a piano in his pajamas late at night with tears streaming down his face singing, "Isn't he beautiful? Beautiful, isn't he?" Worship is an attitude we have been called to share with the body of Christ, not a packaged set of rules and styles that we sell to the highest bidder. Snip, snip. . . .

My Lutheran friend, in turn, shared a time when he asked a group of new members at his church to share their first memory of taking communion. Almost unanimously, the response was about being excluded. What they remembered most clearly was when they were not allowed to participate in the blessing of Christ. Though there might be some doctrinal substantiation for that practice, the message this tradition communicated should be examined. My friend saw that a culture had developed between the haves and the have-nots when it came to receiving Christ's blessings. Snip, snip. . . .

None of us is immune to the disease of conformity. If you're like me, you may tend to see your church as somehow impervious to its infection. To find out the truth, take this simple litmus test. Honestly ask yourself how your house of worship treats:

- ► Smokers versus nonsmokers
- ► People in three-piece suits versus jeans and T-shirts
- ► Homosexuals versus heterosexuals
- ► Seminary grads versus high-school dropouts
- ► Big tithers versus simple givers
- ► Those who speak in tongues versus those who don't
- ► The body-pierced twentysomethings versus the Eddie Bauer edition
- ► Women versus men
- ► Majority ethnic groups versus minority ethnic groups
- ► People who are fluent in Christianese versus those who are just learning

We may not only be talking about open prejudice but unrecognized bias as well. If there is a difference in how people are treated, served, valued, or listened to, I suggest that you have a culture of conformity. Your community is cutting off new life rather than blessing it. If people feel the cost may be too high to reveal who they are in your group, you may have a conformity problem. Even if a person is struggling with sin (sexual sin comes to mind here), he needs someplace in your community where he can tell the truth about this struggle without someone immediately whipping out the pruning shears.

Whenever we feel pressure to conform, we should ask ourselves, *Is this something Jesus would have died for?* This question should be applied to all of our church culture, from the importance of looking culturally hip in church to the type of music we worship with to how we do evangelism. We spend a lot of energy in churches promoting our opinions. Soon our opinions become our creed, our creeds become our dogma, and then we find ourselves walking around with a big pair of pruning shears, looking for people who don't fit our expectations.

If Jesus wouldn't give his life for it, maybe I shouldn't be spending mine on it either. Seriously, do you think Jesus' preference of an organ or a guitar on Sunday morning is what kept him on the cross?

A Letter I Didn't Expect

Of course I believed my tribe, my community, was different. I believed we had conquered that vile demon of conformity. But much of what we see depends on what we're looking for, and I wasn't exactly looking for evidence of conformity in my tribe. A few years ago, after I had been leading a small group for almost a year, I received this letter from a member (we'll call her Cathy):

I don't pretend to know more than you. I don't even pretend to know as much as you. And I especially don't pretend to know you. I would have liked to of gotten to know you, but I don't think that's gonna happen. I tried so hard (maybe too hard) to fit in w/ you and the rest, but I don't. . . . I believe that what you believe makes you who you are. I have not been living what I believe. I've been living what I thought others wanted me to believe. I can't do that anymore. It hurts too much. I guess you could say I've been living a lie. . . . I don't want to believe things just because I think I'm supposed to anymore. I wanna believe them because it means something to me. I want what I believe to make who I am. . . . I'm scared of what I don't believe. I wanna believe things about God but I don't know how.

I'll share the end of the letter with you in a moment, but let's look at this section in the light reflecting off my pruning shears. My first response to this letter was, "Holy cow, I had no idea." All this time with Cathy and she was bottling this stuff up, while I led a group whose supposed purpose was to "try to become more like Jesus."

Cathy had been afraid to ask the hard questions for fear that she would be disqualified from our game. In her eyes, everyone else (including me) had it together. When doubt or desire for transparency began to bud, something was happening to cut that life off. (Yes, I believe even doubt can bring forth life when it is allowed expression.) Her conclusion was that there must be something wrong with her heart.

Had my group created a culture of conformity instead of one of exploration and diversity? Had my leadership unintentionally produced an environment where people felt pressured to seem more "spiritually together" than they were? Had I handed our pruning shears to others without knowing it?

It happens all the time in church groups. We esteem the standards of Scripture, communicate a morality far above that which most of us actually live, and encourage (perhaps even pressure) each other to be more Christlike. Then the Enemy works his subtle scheme. One day I looked in the mirror and realized that my halo was a bit tainted because of poor choices I had made. Simultaneously, a voice in my head convinced me that the price of confession is too high. I rationalized putting on the mask of spiritual aptitude with thoughts like:

> ▸ *I don't want to disappoint my friends.*
> ▸ *As a leader, I don't want them to stumble. I have a responsibility to model a Christlike standard.*
> ▸ *It's really not that big of a deal. I'll fix it myself.*
> ▸ *I need their acceptance, not their rejection.*
> ▸ *What if my family finds out?*

I wondered if my small group had transformed into such a place. The rest of Cathy's letter gave me permission to find out:

> I decided to tell you because you're my friend and I know that you've been there for me. I'm not sure what this is gonna do in the long run as far as if I'll still be at church and Bible study, but for right now, I know that if I keep going to them, some of my questions might get answered. I hope this won't change our friendship.

Cathy, my wife, and I met later that week for coffee and talked about her letter. We said we accepted her unconditionally and gave her permission to wonder and search for genuine faith. But the nagging question in my heart continued: *How would my small group respond if they knew what I knew about Cathy?* I asked her if she would be willing to come to the group and let me read her letter. I told her, "You and I both need to know if this is a safe place to ask the hard questions."

The reading of the letter was a breakthrough not only for Cathy but also for our entire group. There was no hint of shame or rejection but instead an outpouring of love and relief. We learned that when one person starts to live under the rules of conformity, another will join, and then another and another until a whole culture of conformity develops.

Freedom on the Horizontal and Vertical

The good news is that the same can be true of transparency. When one person gets honest, it unleashes a flood of freedom that allows people to be real both on the horizontal with people and the vertical with Jesus. New life sprouted not only in Cathy but the rest of us as well!

It can be risky to be real with a group, but pretending and genuineness are not compatible lifestyles. Like Cathy, we must get to a point in which the risk of rejection by those who profess to care is outweighed by the reward of acceptance by those who really do. Making a choice like that can determine whether we grow to be bonsai believers or become the thriving trees God desires.

How subtly the bonsai life can come upon us. We learn to live on so little nutrition and allow ourselves to be shaped into something God never intended. But to become truly Christlike in our attitudes, beliefs, and actions, we need more than that. Some of us might turn out more weathered-looking than others, but at least when people see us, they will recognize a real person, with real fruit, and the real kingdom life growing within. Of course, real fruit and foliage also attract some nasty critters.

GROWTH POINTS

1. Is your community of faith a safe or unsafe place to share the dark side of your life? What qualities make you see it that way? How do you contribute to that very culture?

2. What would happen if you went against the grain this Sunday at church? What if you wore jeans instead of dress clothes? Wore a tie instead of a T-shirt? Sat in a different seat? Responded with more than "fine" when someone asked, "How are you?" Are you willing to try it?

CHAPTER 8

PUSH
THROUGH
PAIN

THE CALL CAME TO my house late one night as I was making my final approach for a crash landing after a busy Sunday. I had cruised through two morning services and a new-members class, and I finally had the opportunity to snuggle on the couch with my wife. As I stared at the unrecognized number on my caller ID, I went through a mental ping-pong match. I knew I had only four rings before my voice mail picked up. Should I answer or not? This time I did.

"Hello. This is Eric."

"Pastor Eric. My name's Jim. You don't know me, because I attend another church in the area. But I know you guys believe in praying for the sick, and I haven't needed to believe in it till now. Would you please come pray for my wife, Lynn? She's dying."

The desperation in his voice tore at my already tired soul. After a little more dialogue and a nod of approval from my wife, I agreed to head over. I knew God was up to something, but I didn't know what.

When I arrived, God's story unfolded. I saw that hospice had once again done a superb job at making this tiny home a place of peace. Two small children sat quietly in the living room, eyes glazed over from fear and tiredness, while Jim escorted me to the bedroom. The room smelled of death and disease; Lynn's body was ravaged by cancer. She teetered on the last hours of life.

This is a job for Saint Francis of Assisi, not me, Lord, I thought.

Jim begged, "Please pray that God would heal my wife. I know he caused this so that we would grow in our faith, but I don't want my kids' faith to have to grow this way."

My heart sank as my brain registered what I had just heard. I can't imagine how painful that statement must have been to God. It was hard for me to contain the rage toward whoever had taught him such garbage and simultaneously speak with compassion to him. Suddenly, I knew I had been called upon to be a minister of healing not to his wife but to Jim and his kids. God wanted to heal their wounded hearts. And that evening as we helped Lynn pass on to eternal life with Jesus, that same Savior brought abundant life to them.

Perhaps I'll step on some doctrinal toes here, but I'm not a proponent of the bunk that says, "Oh, just rejoice, brother. God must have caused this to happen for your strengthening." If you have ever sat and looked into the eyes of a heartbroken father whose wife just died of cancer, leaving behind two small children, you'll know why I feel this way.

I just can't tell someone God would take a mother from her children just to teach them a life lesson. Nor do I serve a sadistic God who would take a child from a parent just so he can "have another flower in his garden." I live in the real world of brokenness, sin, and pain. God entered into this world of hurt and gave life so that I can know what Paul knew:

For I am convinced that neither death nor life, neither angels nor demons, neither the present nor the future, nor any powers, neither height nor depth, nor anything else in all creation, will be able to separate us from the love of God that is in Christ Jesus our Lord. (Romans 8:38-39)

I serve a loving God, not one who would inflict pain on his children just to challenge them to grow. God never promised that nothing bad would happen to us—we live in a fallen world. There is no promise that just coming to Jesus will make every day sunny and every night peaceful. I know Jesus, yet my car still breaks down, my kids throw up on Saturday nights, close friends die of cancer, and my dog pees on my carpet. It rains on the just and unjust alike, but that doesn't mean God is up there in heaven inflicting this bad stuff on us and saying, "It's for your own good."

The difference between bonsai believers and real ones is in how we look at adversity and how we look at God in the midst of it. Bonsai believers avoid facing adversity because it destroys them. Real-world followers of Christ push through loss because it refines them. They can do this because of who they know God is.

Dog-Gone Painful

As a father, I wouldn't shoot my own kid's beloved dog just to teach her some bizarre lesson regarding the circle of life. That would be cruel. And my Father in heaven has more perfect love than I have. However, life happens and my kids have lost a dog.

Our family was spending an afternoon together on a rare sunny Pacific Northwest day. Tragedy struck: Our normally outdoor-savvy dog got too curious and too close to an ocean cliff, and fell.

I cannot describe for you the pain I felt for my children as I held them and told them what had happened. They didn't blame me for his death, but they held on to me in order to gain life and perspective. Their pain was real (as was mine), and we didn't try to bury or candy-coat it. Instead, in the arms of love, they grew to understand it and cherish the gifts God gives us a little more. Life had happened, and a lesson was there to be learned.

The problem is, many of us don't take time to seek Jesus as the Master of Life and ask him what can be learned from pain. We attend our houses of worship and Band-Aid ourselves just enough so others can't see us bleeding. Then we sing, "Halleluiah, praise the Lord" a few times and go home. But the pain is still there, nagging us like a splinter lodged beneath a fingernail. Perhaps a few pills or a glass of wine will numb it enough. Maybe a few hours on the Internet or a trip to the mall will do. Anything to numb the pain—anything but you, Jesus.

Recently I consulted one of the physical trainers in my gym because my right shoulder was aching all the time and was hindering my ability to work out. I explained my symptoms to the trainer, and she responded with some wise words: "Yep. There must be something wrong with your shoulder that's making it hurt."

Before you write her off as a trainer who got her degree out of a Cracker Jack box, you need to see the wisdom in her diagnosis. Many of us today forget that pain exists for a reason. It is there to tell us something is wrong. For many of us, *pain becomes the problem* we are trying to fix, and we forget to look deeper into its source. We try so hard to protect ourselves from life's struggles that we make ourselves weaker.

Again, the bonsai analogy is helpful. It turns out that the two biggest threats to a bonsai are pests and adverse weather. A tree so delicately shaped and starved can't withstand attack from insects or parasites. Even a shift in temperature or precipitation that would not faze even a sickly outdoor tree can irreparably damage or kill a bonsai. Therefore, it must be protected from anything that may inflict stress upon it. Get this: Bonsai are designed to look like they have weathered the harshest of elements, even though in reality they never have or could!

That's not how we are called to live as followers of Christ. God never promised that nothing bad would happen to us. Again, the difference between bonsai believers and thriving ones is not that we are protected from crisis but that we are equipped for it!

God's Armor

Paul wrote, "Finally, be strong in the Lord and in his mighty power. Put on the full armor of God so that you can take your stand against the devil's schemes" (Ephesians 6:10-11). Why would Paul tell us to put on armor if something bad wasn't going to happen? And where does he ever say to take it off?

I know people who talk about needing to put on the armor of God every time something negative happens. Shouldn't we always be equipped with the armor, especially if the strong biblical case is correct that the armor is Jesus himself? Becoming a follower of Christ is a daily (and nightly) lifestyle, not just a piece of equipment I put on in a crisis, like a gas mask for worst-case scenarios or flea repellent for life's pesky annoyances.

Through Christ Jesus, we have already received victory over sin and destruction. We don't need to fight to survive. Yet we still need Christ's armor because although the outcome is inevitable, so is the battle in the meantime. And merely avoiding sin isn't enough.

Bonsai believers try to avoid battle. Life continues to happen, but we either anesthetize ourselves so heavily that we no longer feel it, or we shut our eyes and quote Scripture verses, hoping it will go away. Instead of understanding that all fruit in the kingdom is bitter before it's ripe, we settle for plastic, coffee-table fruit that only looks real.

A stroll through Wal-Mart's medicine aisles convinced me that we live in a culture of anesthetists. As I slurp a double Americano to keep my headache at bay, let me tell you what I saw. Ten pain medicines had "maximum strength," and a few even had "new and improved maximum strength." What does that mean? Maximum strength—is that the most a human body can handle? If I took just a little bit extra, would my head explode or would I go into a coma? It seems that everything for alleviating our pain is either maximum strength, longer lasting, new and improved, or fast acting.

I understand that. When I have pain—whether in my head, neck, back, or wherever—I want relief and I *want it now!* As a culture, we spend billions treating the physical symptoms of pain and then double that again as we drink and crank away our emotional ones. Pain is bad; relief is good.

The irony is that no part of the fruit of the Spirit will grow in our lives outside of adversity. I say "part" of the fruit of the Spirit because Paul referred to all the qualities of the Spirit-led life as *one* fruit: "But the fruit of the Spirit is love, joy, peace, patience, kindness, goodness, faithfulness, gentleness and self-control" (Galatians 5:22-23).

Love has its greatest opportunities to grow in my life when anger or indifference is the preferred option. Joy has so much more power to change me when I give it the preferred place over depression. Christ-given peace is so much more tangible in circumstances that would dictate fear. Kindness and goodness are easy to manifest when others are doing the same, but they're sweeter when given away to someone who is bitter. Self-control is no problem when it comes to abstaining from brussels sprouts, but sit me down in front of a bag of hot buttered popcorn, and I'll know how shallow self-control's roots go in me.

Jars of Treasure

We must learn to find the purpose of our pain. Jesus is drawn to pain. His nature is to show compassion to the wounded who call on him. He is the great healer. When we stop blaming him for our hurt and diseases, we will be able to trust him to hold us and give us life and perspective through them. When we can admit that we live in a fallen world where sin abounds, we will be able to let God's grace abound that much more. Allowing the kingdom of God to grow within us gives us the ability to actually thrive in adversity instead of cower from it.

Take Paul's clay pot illustration: "But we have this treasure in jars of clay to show that this all-surpassing power is from God and not from us. We are hard pressed on every side, but not crushed; perplexed, but not in despair" (2 Corinthians 4:7-8).

Paul said we are destined for hard times. How can a weak vessel withstand such an onslaught of pressure, perplexity, and pain? Imagine holding a drinking glass in your hand. Grip and squeeze it (don't try this at home; just use your imagination). What's going to happen? Eventually, it's going to break. The only way a clay pot or glass is not going to break under pressure is if its contents are exerting enough strength from the inside to counter what is happening on the outside. Jesus followers should have the kingdom of God permeating them so much that it gives them strength when they feel weak, sight when they feel blind, direction when they feel lost, and comfort when they feel abandoned.

What we profess aloud is often as trite as a beauty queen at a

Miss Whatever pageant: "If I could have any wish, I would wish for world peace and an end to disease and hunger for the world's children." The truth is, most of us just want our pain stopped and our own hunger sated. Jesus could do it. He could just say, "Shazam!" and make all of our hurts go away.

But it's God's story, not ours. His story is about redemption, about bringing everything back under his loving purpose. Most of us know the end of the story and want it now, but we live in the active present-future of what God is doing. We are in the closing moments of God's story of redemption and healing. At the cross, Jesus invaded history and unleashed the cure for the poison that flows through humanity's veins. Still, the consequences of our actions haunt us every time we visit a hospital, turn on the evening news, or see the homeless on the streets. God is sovereign and good, yet he allows suffering. When the paradox spins in our limited minds, we regain our focus by staring at the cross. Jesus has been there.

Truth or Circumstances

Understanding the difference between truth and circumstances can take us a long way in our ability to weather life's storms. At any point, we can look at our circumstances. When circumstances are going well, we often feel like we are walking in God's good graces. My job is wonderful, my spouse thinks I'm sexy and smart, my kids view me as a hero, and I actually won something more than free french fries in the latest McDonald's prize giveaway. Clearly God is blessing my faithfulness. He loves me so much.

Then the tide goes out. Things change and satisfaction dissipates. I get a bad evaluation at work, my spouse asks if I'm gaining weight, or my kids think I'm a dork because I listen to eighties music. I begin to wonder where God's love is in my life. Then the unthinkable happens: cancer, death of a loved one, career crash. *Where are you God? Don't you care about me? What did I do wrong? Don't you love me anymore?* I begin to perceive truth through my circumstances. Circumstances become the lenses through which I see God. But since when do my circumstances determine how much God cares about me? The truth is that his love never changes. The truth is that he is faithful and merciful—always. The truth is that God has the ability to work all things out for good for those who love him. He doesn't cause all things to happen but works through all things that do happen.

When circumstances dictate how I perceive God's truth, my soul and faith shrink when things aren't going well. I quote lots of Scriptures to convince others that I'm okay, but in reality I'm becoming a bonsai. Instead, I must learn to interpret my circumstances in light of God's vast love for me, even when I'm sitting in a world of brokenness. Living with the tension between God's sovereignty and this world's brokenness can actually strengthen my branches.

The book of Lamentations is a poem written in response to a horrible tragedy: the destruction of Jerusalem by the Babylonians. Tradition attributes its writing to the prophet Jeremiah, although the book itself never names the author. Like artists throughout history, this poet has an amazing ability to articulate the paradox many of us wrestle with: that of a loving God's sovereignty and our world's brokenness.

Chapter 3 of Lamentations has two distinct sides. Both are about the same circumstances. Woven throughout this broken yet hopeful poet's words is the tension we all get to live with. Bad things continue to happen. Sometimes we bring them on ourselves and sometimes they are brought upon us, but they always occur under God's indisputable love and awareness. First, Jeremiah says,

I am the man who has seen affliction
    by the rod of his wrath.
He has driven me away and made me walk
    in darkness rather than light;
indeed, he has turned his hand against me
    again and again, all day long.
He has made my skin and my flesh grow old
    and has broken my bones.
He has besieged me and surrounded me
    with bitterness and hardship. (Lamentations 3:1-5)

Jeremiah knows pain. He continues to mourn for another *thirteen* verses. He finishes the left side of this chapter (verse 20) with, "And my soul is downcast within me." Then suddenly his perspective shifts. As when the lenses of a pair of binoculars finally come into focus, Jeremiah chooses to let truth bring circumstances into focus. An amazing thing occurs: His circumstances don't change; *he* changes!

Yet this I call to mind
    and therefore I have hope:
Because of the LORD's great love we are not consumed,
    for his compassions never fail.
They are new every morning;
    great is your faithfulness.
I say to myself, "The LORD is my portion;
    therefore I will wait for him."
The LORD is good to those whose hope is in him,
    to the one who seeks him;
it is good to wait quietly
    for the salvation of the LORD. (Lamentations 3:21-26)

Jeremiah chooses truth over circumstances. His spirit lifts, and he grows. Then for *forty* verses, he gains perspective. He sees his pain in the context of a broken world and rebellious sea of humanity. God is not just the cause but also the solution for his problems. His soul is no longer shriveling in self-pity but is thriving in brokenness. And it all started with truth or circumstances.

Just like Jeremiah, we get to choose which side of Lamentations 3 we will live on. On the left side we have despair where circumstances taint the truth about God, while on the right side we have faith and hope that grow when truth puts circumstances into perspective.

You and I can actually grow in the midst of chaos and pain. God doesn't punish Jeremiah's poetic honesty. In fact, he encourages it. His desire is that we wrestle through our feelings with him, because the outcome is honesty with God. Jesus was born into the harshest of environments in order to help us learn how to walk in harmony with God's kingdom regardless of our circumstances. That is much easier said than done, but Jesus never promised it would be easy—only possible. We don't have to live shielded lives. Storms can actually make us healthier and stronger.

The bonsai, because it has been protected so much, can be irreparably hurt by even a minor attack from a pest or slight exposure to adverse weather. The same doesn't have to be true for our souls.

GROWTH POINTS

1. Write down a few of the most painful things you ever have had to endure. It may not be easy, but revisit those moments and choose to believe God's love was there. How do you think he was feeling, knowing how sin ravages humanity in times like you experienced?

2. We all have pain. We all anesthetize it in various ways. What do you do?

3. Do you know the source of your various hurts? Sometimes physical pain is symptomatic of spiritual or emotional hurts. Make a timeline of your life emotionally and physically. If physical pain shows up within six months of an emotional hurt, pray to understand if there is a connection.

CHAPTER 9

THE LAUNCHED LIFE

"Hey, Harry. You know we are sitting on four million pounds of fuel, one nuclear weapon, and a thing with 270,000 moving parts—built by the lowest bidder. Makes you feel good, don't it?"

—*ARMAGEDDON*

MY FRIEND AND I were watching the movie *Armageddon* on his big screen with full DTS surround sound. The space shuttles were launching. Blue smoke poured from the base of the rockets, and the walls of the room vibrated with the awesome resonance of fifteen hundred watts of digital power. Then my friend hit the pause button, and everything froze. He said, "You know, it's not really like that." He went on to explain his experience watching the launch of the real space shuttle.

Apparently, people sit on the bleachers almost two miles away from the launch site, waiting for the final countdown. They hear the man in mission control counting down in sync to the giant digital clock: "Three, two, one, liftoff!" Smoke billows from the rocket, the nearly blinding orange light from the intense rocket flames ignites, and everything is illuminated with light. Yet there is silence—yes, silence.

Then suddenly, a huge rolling wave of sound overtakes what's left of your senses. Everything rumbles stronger and stronger. You feel incredible awe and amazement as the shuttle rises slowly into the air. When it's just a speck in the sky, an intense blue flame appears. Then the shuttle disappears as it blends in to the sky.

After receiving my physics lesson regarding the sensation chasm between the speed of light and the speed of sound, my friend hit play on the remote. The room vibrated again as the rocket engines fired, and despite his attempt to educate me in Hollywood's lack of realism, I was once again immersed in the experience. Still, it got me pondering the purpose of viewing such a launch. I now wonder whether people who attend the real thing go home afterward saying, "Well, that was a great launch! Now, what's for dinner?"

What I'm really asking is, *Is all that billowing smoke, thunderous sound, and intense light just to entertain us?*

Of course not. NASA doesn't spend gazillions of dollars just to put on a show for those space groupies in the bleachers. They are launching a mission. Each time the space shuttle leaves earth, it does so with a purpose. In light of the tragedies of the space shuttles Challenger and Columbia, I wonder if, for many onlookers, part of the excitement of watching the launch is wondering whether or not the mission will be a success.

In a similar way, as the pastor of a church, I sometimes wonder why we put so much effort into a Sunday-morning experience. The norm for many churches today is that nearly 80 percent of their budget (building, staff, and materials) is dedicated to 20 percent of their time (a Sunday service and perhaps a midweek service). We work really hard to provide a meaningful worship experience. But we must ask, "For what reason?" Is it merely with the hope that they will return for the encore next week?

Churches like mine consistently have powerful worship services. Many tangibly feel God's presence and majesty. Some Sundays are powerful encounters, like watching the space shuttle launch. On any given Sunday, hundreds of people may attend to watch the spectacle and feel the energy. But also, as with a launch, I know that the experience is not supposed to be all there is. There needs to be a greater mission besides just entertaining the people in the bleachers.

When I watch *Armageddon,* I have a transcendent experience of sorts. I enter another world. At certain parts I find my adrenaline pumping, while during others I shed a few tears and even get a bit sleepy. That's not unlike a typical Sunday-morning experience for many of us. But a true worship experience should be more than an adrenaline rush. Like the real shuttle, its mission is far larger than mere entertainment. True worship experiences should launch us into things that would otherwise never happen!

When I leave from an encounter with God, shouldn't the experience be more life-changing than when I watch a really good movie?

Of course it should. But we must honestly ask ourselves, *Is it?* Once again we face the bonsai dilemma. Do we want our worship experiences to be more than bouncing from event to event? Do we want to see meaningful change in our lives? I believe God must have a purpose beyond just entertaining us before he takes us home. Though there are lots of great books on worship, the Master Jesus introduced me first to the prophet Isaiah, who had experienced life-changing worship.

If you could look in the margin of my Bible, you would see some scribble notes next to Isaiah 6. To this day, I'm not sure who was the teacher who caused my hand to scribble so fast. This passage depicts one of the greatest worship experiences ever recorded, as God launched Isaiah into his mission: building God's kingdom into others' lives. I've concluded that one of the crucial nutrients of genuine life in Christ is simply: worship.

Isaiah described a worship experience that would put a cranked-up, full-blown, Dolby DTS/THX DVD performance on HDTV to shame. He said,

> I saw the Lord seated on a throne, high and exalted,
> and the train of his robe filled the temple. Above him
> were seraphs, each with six wings: With two wings
> they covered their faces, with two they covered their
> feet, and with two they were flying. And they were
> calling to one another:
>
> "Holy, holy, holy is the LORD Almighty;
>   the whole earth is full of his glory."
>
> At the sound of their voices the doorposts and thresh-
> olds shook and the temple was filled with smoke.
> (Isaiah 6:1-4)

This wasn't a Spielberg-induced trance; Isaiah was experiencing the real deal. Worship to the max. It was a no-holds-barred, total immersion into the presence of God.

Isaiah saw incredible creatures flying around. He felt the rush of wind as they flapped their wings. His eardrums echoed as they proclaimed, "Holy, holy, holy." He smelled and felt sensations his body had never encountered before. The presence of God Almighty was even making his bones resonate with life. Yet it was all pointing toward something even greater.

God had four things to accomplish. He wasn't just putting on a nice show for Isaiah. Four stages needed to occur in order to launch Isaiah's spirit into the stratosphere while his feet stayed on the terra firma of humanity. Isaiah beckons us to follow him.

Stage 1: See the Awesomeness of Your God

Stage 1 of the launched life is to see God's awesomeness. We should spend time with Jesus every day until we are overwhelmed with his presence. Part of what should happen is that we learn to magnify the Lord. God's presence should get so close to our faces that when we leave our time of worship, we can't help but see him everywhere.

When you put this book down and continue on your journey, will you so magnify the Lord that you see God's craftsmanship in other people, his creative character in nature, his compassion toward those in poverty, and even his love through the dreams that fill your head?

I love this often-quoted statement by Benjamin Warfield: "A glass window stands before us. We raise our eyes and see the glass; we note its quality, and observe its defects; we speculate on its composition. Or we look straight through it on the great prospect of land and sea and sky beyond."[1]

We must train our eyes beyond seeing worship services or Bible studies as ways to make us more knowledgeable about God but no closer to him. Worship and the Word are not just events on Sundays—they are an attitude that so magnifies God that we see Jesus involved in everything! We must purposely look for the story he is writing around us.

I can learn to magnify certain aspects of God's character so his nature becomes easy to see in the world around me.

GOD'S COMPASSION BECOMES EVIDENT EVEN IN TRAGEDY.

I can remember photos of fire department chaplain Mychal F. Judge administering last rites over victims as the World Trade Center towers fell.[2] Like the love of God, he was drawn into the disaster to rescue souls and provide comfort even though human instinct may have been to run away and find protection. Compassion for others cost him his life, just as it did for the Christ he served.

GOD'S MERCY BECOMES EVIDENT EVEN IN HOSTILITY.

The caption of the 1998 *Life* magazine photo reads, "A place where mercy dwells." The photo is of people in the school hallway not long after Michael Carneal shot eight schoolmates in West Paducah, Kentucky. Why mercy? Because not far from the school hung a sign put up by some community members that read, "We forgive you, because God forgave us."[3]

GOD'S HEALING POWER BECOMES EVIDENT EVEN IN A HOSPITAL ONCOLOGY WARD.

Only through God's creative hand do we have the ability to grieve and rejoice simultaneously. My uncle passed away recently under the sudden onslaught of cancer. Yet despair was coupled with rejoicing as I saw God answer one of his life dreams by providing time for him to get married just two months before his journey to heaven. God healed his lonely heart, which had suffered much more pain than his bone cancer would ever cause. To the end, all he could say was, "I'm blessed. I'm very, very blessed."

GOD'S SEARCHLIGHT BECOMES EVIDENT AS HE IS MAGNIFIED AND MY HEART IS EXPOSED.

The light of God has often shined so brightly during private worship time that it also illuminated the darker areas of my soul. Only the presence of Jesus can reveal places where pride has crept into my attitudes or bitterness is poisoning a relationship. There he is, even in the darkness of my life. I've found it very difficult to be honest in my worship of Christ while simultaneously being defensive and critical in my relationship with my wife. As I magnify my relationship with Jesus, he magnifies my relationships with others.

"Oh, Jesus, help me to see you in everything." That type of prayer doesn't seek to make him the cause of all things that happen. Instead, it acknowledges him as present and available to teach apprentices (like you and me) something about everything that does happen. But if we are not seeking to magnify the Lord in the smaller things of life, we most likely will not see him in the powerful ones either.

Stage 2: See the Ugliness of Your Sin

The second stage in a launched life is to see the ugliness of your sin. It's one thing to magnify Jesus so that I see him in everything and quite another to let him see everything in me. Notice Isaiah's response to that incredible worship event: "'Woe to me!' I cried. 'I am ruined! For I am a man of unclean lips, and I live among a people of unclean lips, and my eyes have seen the King, the LORD Almighty'" (Isaiah 6:5).

Brother Isaiah didn't feel like partying in God's presence. Instead, the more the Lord was magnified, the smaller he felt. Oh, those nasty lips of Isaiah. His speaking ability was not only a gift but also a weakness. As the magnification came, he knew just where he was guilty. Isaiah didn't sidestep the conviction or minimize the sin. Whoa or Woe—either way, you and I need a "whoa-woe" time in our pursuit of Jesus.

Whoa: Stop for a moment and admit not only that you are a sinner (in theory) but honestly how you have grievously sinned this week. Woe: Admit how bad sin really is. Let's not just admit we all sin but fess up to the damage it causes. I sinned today, period.

Author Brennan Manning has taught me not to hide the ways in which my halo is tilted:

> At Sunday worship, as in every dimension of our existence, many of us *pretend to believe* we are sinners. Consequently, all we can do is pretend to believe we have been forgiven. As a result, our whole spiritual life is pseudo-repentance and pseudo-bliss. . . . The spiritual future of ragamuffins consists not in disavowing that we are sinners but in accepting that truth with growing clarity, rejoicing in God's incredible longing to rescue us in spite of everything.[4]

Perhaps there is no bigger barrier to being a genuine person of faith than secrets. We can't keep hiding those dark areas of sin and struggle from Jesus our Master and those around us whom we call friends. Intimacy requires transparency. So, will the real sinners please stand up?

As I stare at my computer screen, I am reminded of what a friend and enemy this Pentium-powered beast has become to me over the years. Sometimes I can't believe how the simple DSL cable that plugs into the back of my laptop has brought me an endless buffet of images and struggles. That portal into the Internet has opened up a wormhole of opportunity to both stumble and bless. How could such a small device wield such power over a man of God?

That's the problem: the whole man-of-God thing. For years, I pretended to be something I wasn't. I wasn't just a short guy trying to become more like Jesus. I wasn't desiring to *become* a true follower of Christ while admitting my halo was tilted; instead, I wanted to *already be* a true follower of Christ. Then I needed others to tell me the same. Because my gifts were bearing fruit in ministry, others had little reason to believe I wasn't doing well. But I still carried the secret, and the power of that secret kept me from becoming what I truly wanted to be in the first place.

Soon, however, my gifts found out they were no match for my character (what little I had). I promise that if you don't admit your sins to Jesus and confess them to some trusted friends, they will find their way out of the closet at the most inopportune times. Whoa.

J. Lee Grady, editor of *Charisma* magazine, said that ten of the ministry leaders who graced the cover of his magazine in the 1980s eventually were rocked by embarrassing scandals. As well, six of the mega-churches they featured in an article entitled "Outstanding Churches in America" eventually disbanded because of ethical failures.[5]

You and I are not some super church figures. We are just, well, us. Nonetheless, either authenticity or bonsaihood may be manifested in those great moments of life, but it must be manufactured in the small ones, whether it's just us or a mega-ministry.

I didn't have to watch a multimillion-dollar ministry collapse because the sin I refused to deal with privately was exposed publicly. Instead, I got to endure something worse. Just a few years ago, I felt the breaking of the thing I treasured most in my life: my wife's heart. I got to see the pain in my beloved wife's eyes and hear the rebuke of Jesus for violating a covenant I made with him to love and cherish her till death do us part. It just took a few moments of treating myself to some of Satan's eye candy by surfing the wrong waves on the Internet Ocean. The price was the crushed trust of my beloved. Woe to me, a man of unclean eyes.

So let me jump-start the magnification for you a bit. I am convinced that over 80 percent of Christian men today struggle with one or a combination of these three secrets: (1) homosexuality, (2) pornography, and, dare I say it, (3) masturbation. For women I see a constant struggle with these issues: (1) past hurts from sexual abuse that go unhealed, (2) struggles with body image often manifested through bulimia or anorexia, and (3) hidden but pervasive feelings of anxiety and depression.

I'm not even saying that these things could all necessarily be defined as "sin," but they are too often taboo topics in church circles. They become the hidden monsters that we wrestle with in the dark and expend energy on hiding during the day. They become the hidden wires that shape our identities and keep us from growing in the directions that God has intended.

Can you relate? If so, then ask yourself, *Does anyone know?* When you are around a group of Christians whom you would call your friends, do you fear being discovered? Or has your willingness to admit sin before God enabled you to be transparent before at least a few others?

This second stage of launching our lives toward bona fide faith must include letting Jesus see everything in us, and that often comes through his people. I have found incredible freedom in being transparent about my struggles. Being transparent doesn't justify the sin or the damage it causes, but I have found that most demons lose their power when brought out into the light.

Without the transparency and an I'm-going-to-stop-pretending attitude, we are destined to sin-repent-sin-repent until we are caught or give up on faith entirely. We must come to a place where we let Jesus embrace those dark areas of our souls. Otherwise, those holes in our hearts will keep allowing God's presence to leak out.

That's why we can experience God's presence at church service after church service and then walk out the door and get yanked by the same old secret sin. We know that where God's presence is, there is healing. But if God is not allowed to touch those areas of woundedness in our hearts, his presence cannot remain, and we will feel the healing abandon us. It will just leak out. Bonsai believers learn to live on the minimum of God's presence. Genuine followers don't.

Those holes in our containers must be fixed. So many sincere Christians can "be filled" with God in one moment and then turn and make decisions motivated by their emptiness and pain the next. We must honestly declare our need for healing if we are going to live the life we desire.

Stage 3: Experience God's Cleansing

When Isaiah confessed how small and dirty he was compared to such a wonderful, powerful, and awesome God, he reached stage three of a launched life: repentance and cleansing. For Isaiah, repentance seemed to have something to do with his mouth. Whatever repentance involves for you, it's a reexamination of yourself in light of what you have just seen or experienced. Like Isaiah, we say, "Lord, I'm a mess. Look at my life. Please come and cleanse me, because by myself I can't do it."

Then, because of his shed blood on the cross, Jesus can set you right again with God. I have experienced that forgiveness through feeling my burdens lifted during personal encounters with Christ and through the acceptance of those who I felt would reject me. But I had to get real! Once again, "Will the real sinner please stand up?"

God had to take a hot coal to burn the uncleanliness from Isaiah's lips. I'm sure that hurt, but the freedom that came with it must have been wonderful. We can read any number of commentaries on what the coal signified, but God was willing to do whatever was necessary to cleanse this man because Isaiah had a mission to accomplish. In order to stop the sin-repent-sin-repent cycle, we must decide that continuing to do what we've always done to overcome our demons will only continue to produce what we've always gotten.

Now is the time to take a more radical approach. Seek healing, no matter how much it burns. You and I are not living for other people's approval—we are living for Christ's alone. Even a cursory reading of the gospels shows us that those the Lord Jesus loved, healed, and embraced the most were often the most broken and diseased. Trust me, if you stop minimizing your disease, you will maximize your healing.

Stage 4: See God's Purposes Active in Your Life

Isaiah's worship path led him to one last stage. God used his incredible experience to launch him into a greater mission than he ever could have imagined! In the same way, God wants to take you and me from worship, to repentance, through healing, to his ultimate purpose of rescuing others. We are not just called to *watch* this spiritual rocket launch; we are called to go along for the ride! "Whom shall I send?" God asked. "Send me!" Isaiah answered (see Isaiah 6:8).

Something amazing happens when we see Jesus and experience his cleansing at a deeper level than just an intellectual one. Our fundamental orientation of life turns more to his purposes. Whatever we fix our eyes upon, we will become.

Though not as dramatically as Isaiah, I have seen Jesus my King! He has set my heart right with his heart. As I have magnified him, I now see his involvement in the world around me. I now know the redemptive power of the King, but people who haven't experienced the release and forgiveness that comes from such an encounter surround me every day. *Here I am, Lord. Send me!*

Now that's a complete worship experience, I mean, worship lifestyle. Worship should be the fire and energy that lifts us from where we are to a higher purpose than just entertainment.

I Want to Grow!

Bonsai trees really are beautiful works of living art. They are sculptured and meticulously cared for by the gardener. It is simply amazing that a plant designed by God to be so big can be kept so small. But what is success for the bonsai is failure for the believer. Our Creator designed us to start as small as a mustard seed and grow in ways that make people notice the kingdom of God within and through us.

Unfortunately, we don't decide once for all time to be authentic trees and then forget about it. It's a daily adventure and effort. If we wanted safety and simplicity, we'd go back to that little pot indoors, out of the rain. But the voice and presence of Jesus is found out there in the real world with wind, rain, and beautiful sunsets.

For many of us, the desire to be real resonates within us like a distant church bell calling us home, beckoning us further and deeper yet remaining elusive in its attainment. There is a longing in our souls for peace with God and freedom in our relationship with others. We hunger for more of the tangible presence of God as we work out what it means to build a cooperative friendship with Jesus.

We know that just as in the ancient days, there is still as much mystery and adventure as there is security and nurture in a friendship with Jesus. In our growth, we must trust him as the Master Gardener. Some seasons may be long, but our hearts tell us that keeping our tree next to the River of Life will somehow bear much more beauty than pain.

So as you root yourself in Christ, grow in peace and grace, not only toward others but also toward yourself.

GROWTH POINTS

1. Around what would you say your life fundamentally revolves? Is it possible to have your time consumed by career or family and still be oriented toward Christ? Ask him how.

2. Ponder your secrets. Why do you keep them hidden? What would it take to break the sin-repent cycle in your life? Does the burn that brings freedom outweigh the potential burn of embarrassment or reprimand? Is the real you willing to stand up?

NOTES

Chapter 1: BRUTALLY HONEST
1. Gregory of Nyssa, "The Life of Moses," in *Devotional Classics: Selected Readings for Individuals and Groups,* ed. Richard J. Foster and James Bryan Smith (San Francisco: HarperSanFrancisco, 1993), p. 157.

Chapter 3: EMBRACE THE POWER OF COMMUNITY
1. Information about St. David was obtained from www.saintdavid.org.uk and Michael Mitton, *The Soul of Celtic Spirituality: In the Lives of Its Saints* (Mystic, Conn.: Twenty-Third Publications, 1996), pp. 35-41.
2. www.cdc.gov/nchs/releases/01news/trendpreg.htm
3. http://naic.acf.hhs.gov/pubs/s_search.cfm

Chapter 4: ENRICH YOUR SOIL
1. George F. Will, "Seasonal Litigation," *Newsweek* (December 21, 1998), p. 78.
2. "Venisancte Spiritus," *Music from Taizé* (France: Les Presses de Taizé).
3. Help Index, Microsoft Windows ME.

Chapter 5: FEEL THE REIGN

1. Michael Frye, "Be The Centre" (Vineyard Songs, 1999).

2. Brother Lawrence, *The Practice of the Presence of God: With Spiritual Maxims* (Grand Rapids, Mich.: Revell, 2003), pp. 11-13.

3. Brother Lawrence, *The Practice of the Presence of God,* second letter (Grand Rapids, Mich.: Revell, 1967), pp. 36-37.

Chapter 6: UNLEASH YOUR DNA

1. Information about Bernard of Clairvaux was obtained from www.newadvent.org/cathen

2. Philip G. Zimbardo and Richard J. Gerrig, *Psychology and Life,* 15th ed. (N.Y.: Longman, 1999), p. 482.

3. Michael Cole and Sheila R. Cole, *The Development of Children,* 2nd ed. (N.Y.: W. H. Freeman & Co., 1993), p. 361.

4. "Property Laws of a Toddler," www.unr.edu/homepage/shubinsk/toddler.html

5. http://www.corrietenboom.com/history.htm

6. Bernard of Clairvaux, "Four Degrees of Love," in *Devotional Classics: Selected Readings for Individuals and Groups,* ed. Richard J. Foster and James Bryan Smith (San Francisco: HarperSanFrancisco, 1993), p. 40.

Chapter 9: THE LAUNCHED LIFE

1. Benjamin B. Warfield, vol. 1 of *Selected Shorter Writings of Benjamin B. Warfield,* ed. John E. Meeter (Phillipsburg, NJ: Presbyterian and Reformed Publishing Company, 1970), pp. 265-267.

2. www.saintmychal.com/deathof.htm

3. Steve Nagy/The Paducah Sun, "A Place Where Mercy Dwells," photo, *Life* 21, no. 2 (February 1998), p. 12.

4. Brennan Manning, *The Ragamuffin Gospel* (Sisters, Ore.: Multnomah, 1990), p. 136 (emphasis his).

5. J. Lee Grady, "Stop the Sideshows," *Charisma* (January 2002).

ABOUT THE AUTHOR

HAVING RECEIVED HIS PH.D. in Human Development and Family Relations from Oregon State University, Eric Sandras is part of the next generation of leaders whom God is using to "raise the bar" in the relationships, faith, and life decisions of a postmodern generation. He is passionate about family, emergent church issues, and having extra butter on his popcorn at the movie theater. Currently, Eric pastors the Olympic Vineyard Christian Fellowship in Port Angeles, Washington, and still enjoys instructing courses in human sexuality, child development, and psychology at a local university. Eric and Cindy, his wife of fourteen years, have two wonderful children— Dakota Jasmine and Carter William—and a dog named Koki.

SOMETIMES "NAKEDNESS" IS A VIRTUE.

TrueFaced

The attempt to hide our unresolved sin issues is devastating. But God's grace allows us to be who He says we are—true and free. Instead of behaving to please God, we learn our trust pleases Him best.

by Bill Thrall, Bruce McNicol, and John Lynch
1-57683-693-2

Abba's Child

When sin threatens to reveal our imperfect identity, we scramble to appear acceptable by wearing the mask of an impostor. God calls us to put aside the mask and accept our identity as a child of God. *Abba's Child* shows us how.

by Brennan Manning
1-57683-334-8

Dangerous Wonder

If you're looking for the joy and freedom of faith, this book will open your eyes and your life to the exciting adventure of a relationship with God. Now includes a discussion guide.

by Mike Yaconelli
1-57683-481-6

To get your copies, visit your local bookstore,
call 1-800-366-7788, or log on to www.navpress.com.
Ask for a FREE catalog of NavPress products. Offer BPA.

NAVPRESS ®

BRINGING TRUTH TO LIFE
www.navpress.com